Little Laureates

Southern England & The Channel Isles
Edited by Donna Samworth

Young Writers

First published in Great Britain in 2008 by:
Young Writers
Remus House
Coltsfoot Drive
Peterborough
PE2 9JX
Telephone: 01733 890066
Website: www.youngwriters.co.uk

All Rights Reserved

© Copyright Contributors 2007

SB ISBN 978-1 84431 478 2

Foreword

Young Writers was established in 1991 and has been passionately devoted to the promotion of reading and writing in children and young adults ever since. The quest continues today. Young Writers remains as committed to the nurturing of poetic and literary talent as ever.

This year's Young Writers competition has proven as vibrant and dynamic as ever and we are delighted to present a showcase of the best poetry from across the UK and in some cases overseas. Each poem has been selected from a wealth of *Little Laureates* entries before ultimately being published in this, our sixteenth primary school poetry series.

Once again, we have been supremely impressed by the overall quality of the entries we have received. The imagination, energy and creativity which has gone into each young writer's entry made choosing the poems a challenging and often difficult but ultimately hugely rewarding task - the general high standard of the work submitted ensured this opportunity to bring their poetry to a larger appreciative audience.

We sincerely hope you are pleased with this final collection and that you will enjoy *Little Laureates Southern England & The Channel Isles* for many years to come.

Contents

Andrea Pearce (10)   1
Ellen O'Donnell (8)   1

Archbishop Wake Primary School, Blandford

Amie House (10)   2
Gregg Meldrum (9)   2
Nadia Philp (9)   2
Zoe Mansfield (10)   3
Finlay McDonald & Ollie Taylor (10)   3
Lois Yu (9)   3
Chloe Davis (9)   4
Joe Royal (11)   4
Tayef Ali (9)   4
Isabelle Forrest (9)   5
Lewis Shorto (8)   5
Steven Hodgeson (10)   5
Stuart Heckford (10)   6
Joel Mariner (10)   6
Tom Oliver (10)   6
Roya Pomeroy (11)   7
Jake Cotter (9)   7
Rebecca Rowland (10)   7
Tommy Hart (7)   8
May Bailey (7)   8
Ashikur Rahman (10)   8
Kris Jones (7)   9
Miguel Bernabéu (9)   9
Owen Hedicker (9)   9
Emily Park (8)   10
Iona Caines (8)   10
Liam Gonthier (10)   11
Mohena Chowdhury (8)   11
Lucy Brundish (8)   12
Molly Blackwell (9)   12
Bethan Amey (8)   13
Dan Spencer (10)   13
Emily Jones (9)   14
Cameron Wellstead (9)   14

Amy Phillips (9)	14
Ruby Bircham (10)	15
Harun Cakir (10)	15
Kai Williams (8)	15
Samuel Johnson (9)	16
Katherine Stanley (7)	16
Louie Ford (7)	16
Lucy Park (10)	17
Ross Crabbe (9)	17
James Daly (8)	17
Oliver Hooper (10)	18
Sophie Babbs (10)	18
Dustin Gunning-Cole (8)	18
Amy Lillywhite (9)	19
Samantha Critchell (8)	19
Tyler Lanes (8)	19
Alex Cooper (10)	20
Callum Goddard (10)	20
Connor Rosoman (10)	21
Hannah Smith (8)	21
Fern Soda & Kamil Gradzewicz (10)	21
Robert Newitt (10)	22
Samuel Newman (9)	22
Lauren Newman (7)	22
Paige Smith (10)	23
Courtney McCormack (8)	23
Holly Oliver (8)	23
Mackenzie Reid (9)	24
Callum Wray (9)	24

Dover Park Primary School, Ryde

Phebe Seaward (7)	25
Georgia Watts (7)	25
Lucy Grimbley (7)	25
Trinity Magee (7)	26
Jacob Rees (7)	26
Scott Hemming (7)	26

Grouville Primary School, Jersey

Victoria McBoyle (9)	26
Sophie Avant (7)	27

Taryn Pontin (7)	27
Joni Gorman (7)	27
Josephine Carnegie (7)	28
Cerian Mason (8)	28
Emma Wildbore-Hands (9)	29
Isobel Kelly (8)	29
Carys Ingram (9)	30
Amber Smith (10)	30
Uma Le Boutillier (8)	30
Erin & Neve Lynch (8)	31

Mill Rythe Junior School, Hayling Island

Amber Cheverton (9)	31
Jamie Maddison (9)	32
Georgia Rix (9)	33
Georgina Mill (9)	34
Joseph Drayton (9)	35
Megan Capaldi-Tallon (9)	36
Emily Richardson (10)	37
Francesca Ramsbottom (9)	38
David Lasham (9)	39
Euan Condron (9)	40
Libby Dunaway (9)	41
Georgia Tame (9)	42
Bryony Brennan (9)	43
Chloe Bethell (10)	44
Jake Todd (9)	45
Selena Williams (9)	46
Jessica Easton (9)	47
Mia Wick (9)	48

Portway Junior School, Andover

Kieran McHardy & Charlie Rogers (8)	49
Mehgan Skelton (7)	49
Georgia Day (7)	50
Harry Smallbones (7)	50
Connor McMullen & Lewis Coggins (9)	50
Luke Jackson (8)	51
Kingsley Pannell (7)	51
Nathan Birks (7)	51
Chloe Brookes (9) & Lizzie White (8)	52

Jordan Day (8) & Alex Morling (9) 52
Alice Bathie & Kayleigh Morris (8) 53
Dana Shelley (9) & Gabrielle Snook (8) 53
Tayla Moody (8) 54
Luke Holden (8) 54
Siân Allen (9) 55
Cerys Revelle-Scully & Cassie Shearer (8) 55
Jing-Ying Wong & Courtney Tobin (8) 56
Amber Casselton (8) 56
Britney Enright (7) 56

St John's School, Jersey
Scott Gallichan (10) 57
Bryce Leatt (10) 57
Verity Stanier (10) 57
Kealan Bisson (10) 58
Ryan Hillion (10) 58
Jessica Slack (7) 58
Niamh Whiteman (10) 59
Luna Pinto Baker (11) 59
Alice Mitchell (7) 59
Ashton Breen-Faudemer (10) 60
Jack Dorey (10) 60
Bradley Cox (7) 60
Christopher Beynon (10) 61
Harry Lewis (10) 61
Jamie Stewart (7) 61
Jacob Allix (10) 62
Sadie Pinnock (7) 62
Shaynee Whiteman (7) 62
Magdalena Thébault (8) 63
Khaya Pybus (8) 63
Ellie Cooper (7) 63
Sam Masefield (8) 64
Leon Couriard (7) 64
Frankie Jones (7) 64
Mitchell Thebault (8) 65
Ella Averty (7) 65
Jocey Dibbens (8) 65
Henri Helie-Merrony (8) 66
Abbie Roberts (7) 66

Ruby Mason (7)	66
Megan McCabe (8)	67
Daniel Hillion (7)	67
Benjamin Fosse (7)	67
Owen Harper (8)	68
Maxwell Friend (8)	68
Todd Stanier (8)	68
Hannah Couriard (10)	69
Jodie Barry (7)	69
Olivia Bouchard (8)	70
Teigan Purkiss (8)	70
Max Haslam (8)	70

St Luke's Primary School, Jersey

Caitlin Harris (9)	71
Jade McCormack (9)	71
Chloë Portch (9)	71
Sands-Alicia Sangan (10)	72
Mary Melaugh (10)	72
Katie Longman (10)	73
Bradley Welsh-Falle (10)	73
Megan Buxton (10)	74
Taylor Cairns (10)	74
Paige-Aisha Du Feu (10)	75
Caitlin Day (10)	75
Connor Pinel (10)	76
Katie Veitch (10)	76
Keera De Sousa (10)	77
Alex Stout (11)	77
Ella Glasgow (10)	78
Janine McBain (10)	78
Jessica Nelson (10)	78

St Swithun's RC Primary School, Southsea

Martha Noble (9)	79
Jude Keating (9)	79
Jack Yeats (10)	79
Ellie Dommersen (10)	80
Oscar Chase (10)	80
Wiktor Karolewski (10)	80
Freya Hardcastle & Ella Blay (9)	81

Michael Olive (10)	81
Olivia Campion (9)	82
Jessica Cooper (9)	82
Ella Mallinder (9)	82
Lauren Nicholls (10)	83
Isobel Johnson (10)	83
Joshua Humphries & Michael Cox-Smith (11)	84
Elysia Gill (11) & Darcy Leake (10)	85
Grace Goble (10)	86
Hermione Green (10)	87
Guy Elder (10)	88
Samuel Madden (9)	89
Alice Chatband (11)	90
Thomas Rix (9)	90
Peter Jacobs (9)	91
Emilie Duda (10)	91
Louis Lawson (9)	92
Alex Fowler (10)	92
Chloe Hinton (10)	93
Angela Gorman (9)	93
Hannah Haughey (10)	94
Francy Augustine (9)	94
Jack Hardcastle (11)	95
Molly McMaster (9)	95
Christopher Shore (9)	96
Josephine Lake (9)	96
Emma Ford (10)	97
Anita Ghosh (9)	98
Harry Burn (9)	99
Azzurra Moores (9)	100
Carolina Gonzalez (10)	101
Ellie Langton (9) & Gillian	102
Joshua Cooper (10)	103
Naima Reza (10)	104
George Gooding (9)	105
Kiera Quickfall (10)	106
Daniella Ndzi (9)	107
Oscar Addecott (9)	108
Alba Elezi (10)	109
Jessica Henshaw (9)	110
Selina Briggs (9)	110
Patrick Cregan (9)	111

St Thomas Garnet's School, Bournemouth

Diarmid Becker (10)	111
Georgia MacDonald-Taylor (9)	112
Matthew Landi (8)	112
Eleanor Austin (11)	113
Theodore Jeffries (10)	113
Eva Becker (8)	114
Yasmin Sabih (11)	114
Emile Sabih (8)	114
Kai Groves-Waters (7)	115
Kaan Beskardes (10)	115
Scott Austin (8)	115
Dominic Hughes (10)	116
Rebecca Giddens (10)	116
Taylor Rees-Wilton (10)	116
Jessica Balfour (10)	117
Amelia Wood Power (9)	117
Daniel Tofangsazan (10)	117
Matthew Giddens (10)	118
Piers Verstage (9)	118
Nicholas Beaumont (9)	119
Hibba Herieka (8)	119
Glenn Balfour (7)	120
Thomas Adams (9)	120
Olivia Adams (7)	121
Lily Newton (7)	121
Stephania Robbins (7)	122
Kira Allum (7)	122
Howard Winsten-Korver (7)	122
Aiden O'Sullivan (7)	123
Gina Davis (7)	123
Finlay Padwick (7)	123
Sophie Sawyer (7)	124
Lucy Taylor (7)	124
Jonty Hughes (9)	124
Tallulah Pollard (9)	125
Nikan Motlagh (7)	125

Salway Ash CE (VA) Primary School, Bridport

Findlay Purchase (9)	126
Max Purchase (9)	126

Georgia Walther (7)	126
Jamie Herbert (7)	127

Upton Junior School, Poole

Jamie Rocha (8)	127
Tommy Hughes (8)	127
Jasmin Doe (9)	128
Tara Prince (9)	128
Christopher Masters (8)	129
Eve Collins (8)	129
Seven Mason (8)	130
Luis Hayes (8)	130
Kieran Higson (8)	130
Sam Venner (8)	131
Lewis Fooks (8)	131
Lauren Bown (8)	131
Jamie-Leigh Simpson (9)	132
Ella Upward (8)	132
Ella Smith (10)	133
Rachel King	133
Lewis Kelly (10)	134
Sam Jones (9)	134
Joshua Brewster (9)	135
Kaylee Gunner (9)	135
Catherine Lenton (9)	136
Miles Mitchinson (8)	136
Linus Head (9)	137
Jessica Wyatt (7)	137
Emily Jellett (9)	138
Becky Driscoll (10)	138
Thomas Pike (9)	139
Tamsin Edmondson (8)	139
Katie Tilbury (9)	140
Sophie Phillips (8)	140
James Murray (9)	141
Oscar Head (8)	141
Jonathan Hayward (9)	142
Lacey Cole (8)	142
Samuel Hirons (10)	143
Natalie Baker (8)	143
Savannah Morgan (9)	144

Sian Grey (7)	144
Cameron Wemyss (9)	145
Chantelle Squibb (7)	145
Aaron Sheldon (9)	146
Calum Driver (8)	146
James Jackson (9)	147
Nina Czarnokoza (9)	147
Ross Higson (9)	148
Joe Musselwhite (9)	148
Harvey Nichols (9)	149
Abigail Baker (8)	149
Abigail Smith (9)	150
Maddison Higson (8)	150
Chloe Bennett (9)	151
Zara Benjafield (8)	151
James Craze (10)	152
Molly Lloyd (8)	152
Connel Duffy (8)	153
Stephen Brain (7)	153
Chloe Cole (7)	153
Jessica Upton (7)	154
Kasey Taylor (8)	154
Bryony Hobden (8)	155
Elle-Rose Arnold (8)	155
Jordan Mackenzie (8)	156
Madison Gossling (7)	156
Ashley Pope (8)	157
Morgan Tutt	157
Jordan Fripp (7)	157
Robert Beck (8)	157
Cameron Sinden (8)	158
Daniel Meacham (8)	158

The Poems

Forces

Forces are everywhere,
On the Earth, in our hair,
Friction is the force of grip,
Forces can make things slip,
Gravity keeps you on the ground,
Forces don't make a sound.

Forces are everywhere,
On the Earth, in our hair,
Push, pull, stretch, fall,
Forces are invisible,
Some forces are big and tall,
Sometimes their effects are small.

On the Earth, in our hair,
Forces are *everywhere!*

Andrea Pearce (10)

Bugeyland

I am a colourful marble rolling in the sky
with a twinkling trail trailing behind me.
My lakes are made of strawberry milkshake
where the fish swim freely.
I am squidgy like jelly covering the frog-like aliens.
My body, made of colourful rock, is hot fire
so no human can go on me.
I am the most amazing planet in the universe.
My colourful rocks have pretty patterns on.

Ellen O'Donnell (8)

Anger!

The colour of anger is red
It sounds like a cow
Anger tastes like chewing gum
It smells of smoke and petrol
Anger looks like a red devil
Anger feels like a cow being mad and
A kettle steaming in your face
Anger reminds me of a wrecked car that's red
And smashed up by some people in a garage.

Amie House (10)
Archbishop Wake Primary School, Blandford

Happiness

Happiness is like a friend
It sounds like birds tweeting in the trees
It tastes like Scottish shortbread with Christmas sprinkles
It smells like chocolate cake
It looks like children playing in the field
It feels like the fur of a dog
It reminds me of the morning sun.

Gregg Meldrum (9)
Archbishop Wake Primary School, Blandford

Happiness

Happiness is yellow like the sun
It sounds like the laughter of children playing
It tastes like sweet chocolate
Happiness feels ever so nice
Happiness reminds me of Swanage
And having fun in the sun.

Nadia Philp (9)
Archbishop Wake Primary School, Blandford

Anger

The colour of anger is red
It sounds like a cow
It tastes of chewing gum
Anger smells of smoke and a zooming car
Anger looks like a red devil
Anger feels like a kettle steaming through your head
And a cow being mad
Anger reminds me of a wrecked up car that is red.

Zoe Mansfield (10)
Archbishop Wake Primary School, Blandford

Sadness

Sadness is grey like blinding mist.
It sounds like a baby.
It tastes like a salty sea.
It smells like a skunk.
Sadness looks like tears of children.
It feels like no one likes you.
Sadness feels like children who lost someone they loved.

Finlay McDonald & Ollie Taylor (10)
Archbishop Wake Primary School, Blandford

Fear

Fear is black like a dark night sky
It sounds like teeth clattering together
Fear tastes like water swallowed down in one gulp
It smells like nothing in the breeze
It looks like a blank, white picture on a dirty wall
Fear reminds me of a relative in danger!

Lois Yu (9)
Archbishop Wake Primary School, Blandford

Happiness

Happiness sounds like laughter from children.
It is the colour of the deep blue sea at the beach.
It tastes like ice cream on a hot day.
It smells like a sweet shop as you just walk in.
Happiness feels like someone taking you to a place you have
                                            always wanted to go.
Happiness reminds me of when I achieve something.

Chloe Davis (9)
Archbishop Wake Primary School, Blandford

Silence

Silence smells like a gentle brush.
Silence feels like nothing.
Silence reminds me of bedtime.
Silence tastes like a bitter wine.
Silence is a dispersing blank.
Silence looks like a horrid ride.
Silence sounds like nothing.

Joe Royal (11)
Archbishop Wake Primary School, Blandford

Silence

Silence sounds like nothing
Silence tastes of nothing
Silence smells like wind
Silence feels like air
Silence reminds me of quiet
Silence doesn't have a colour
Silence looks like nothing.

Tayef Ali (9)
Archbishop Wake Primary School, Blandford

Fear!

Fear is grey, like in the dull, dark winter night.
Fear sounds like a drip, drip, drip from the cold, freezing tap.
Fear tastes like your last drink of frozen water.
Fear smells like a bonfire in the cold night.
Fear feels like a cold knife in a new heart.
Fear looks like when you're all alone and no one can hear you.
It reminds me of . . .

Isabelle Forrest (9)
Archbishop Wake Primary School, Blandford

Colour Poem

Red is a soft jumper
Orange is bright paints
Yellow is the red-hot sun
Green is the trees blowing in the breeze
Blue is the endless sky
Purple is a warm coat
Black is a sparkly pen
White is a whiteboard.

Lewis Shorto (8)
Archbishop Wake Primary School, Blandford

Anger

Anger is black
It sounds like seafaring
It tastes like sorrow
It smells like badness
It looks like darkness
It feels like hate.

Steven Hodgeson (10)
Archbishop Wake Primary School, Blandford

Fear!

Fear is as black as the night sky,
Fear sounds like a wolf howling at the bright, full moon,
It tastes like a yellow, sour lemon,
Fear smells like a burning hot fire rich in smoke,
Fear looks like a dark, shadowy figure in the moonlight,
Fear feels like a great big, gloopy puddle of black tar,
Fear reminds me of the pitch darkness of a tunnel.
What does fear remind you of?

Stuart Heckford (10)
Archbishop Wake Primary School, Blandford

Sadness

Sadness is a cold, blue teardrop
It sounds like a wailing child
It tastes like a whirlpool of polluted water
Sadness smells like a great rubbish dump
It looks like a bleeding man lying in an alley
It feels like you're trapped in a cage
Sadness is a war memory and a black and white photograph
Sadness is . . .

Joel Mariner (10)
Archbishop Wake Primary School, Blandford

Sadness

Sadness is a sad puddle of blue
It sounds like a newborn baby crying its heart out
It tastes like the sea, salty
It smells like a rotten piece of meat
It looks like a group of people gathered for a funeral
It feels like there's no meaning for you to live
It reminds you of someone you love who just died.

Tom Oliver (10)
Archbishop Wake Primary School, Blandford

Sadness

Sadness is as crystal clear as a falling tear,
It sounds like the whimpering of a severely bitten Yorkshire terrier,
Sadness tastes like the salty bitterness of a tear
splashing on the ground,
Its smell is that of a dark, damp cave on the seashore,
Sadness looks like that small child who is still close to your heart,
It feels as depressing as when no one will listen
to your side of the story,
Sadness reminds you of . . .?

Roya Pomeroy (11)
Archbishop Wake Primary School, Blandford

Fear!

Fear is black and grey, like the middle of the night.
It sounds like a wolf howling in the dead of night.
It tastes like rotten eggs at midnight.
I think it smells like bad breath from a wolf.
When I'm scared it looks like a dead child with a knife in them.
Fear feels like I'm getting beaten up.
It reminds me of getting lost at my friend's birthday party at Bowlplex.

Jake Cotter (9)
Archbishop Wake Primary School, Blandford

Sadness

Sadness is like a grey, gloomy sky,
It sounds like crying from a young child,
It tastes like salty water from the sea,
It smells like freshly cut grass in summer,
Sadness looks like a load crowded at a funeral,
It feels like sitting on a red ants' nest,
Sadness reminds me of . . .

Rebecca Rowland (10)
Archbishop Wake Primary School, Blandford

Colours

Red is my school jumper
Orange is a bright bunch of carrots
Yellow is for a sour lemon
Green is a field of grass
Blue is the calm sea
Purple is for violet flowers
Black is my bedroom at night
White is for plain paper.

Tommy Hart (7)
Archbishop Wake Primary School, Blandford

Colour Poem

Red is a floppy poppy
Orange is a shining sun
Yellow is a big, beautiful sunflower
Green is a tall, leafy tree
Blue is the calm sky
Purple is a sparkling flower
Black is a gloomy spaceship
White is a glistening board.

May Bailey (7)
Archbishop Wake Primary School, Blandford

Anger

Anger is black as the night
Anger is loud as Mum and Dad shouting
Anger tastes like blood when someone is stabbed
It smells like badness.

Ashikur Rahman (10)
Archbishop Wake Primary School, Blandford

Colour Poem

Red is for attractive roses
Orange is for lovely light
Yellow is for a big, sparkling banana
Green is for brilliant leaves
Blue is for giant geraniums
Purple is for beautiful, glamorous dresses
Black is for big, shiny cars
White is for thousands of tiny clouds.

Kris Jones (7)
Archbishop Wake Primary School, Blandford

The Football Match

Bang, the match starts
The crowd as hot as lava
Crash! The ball hits the back of the net
And the pressure melts down
Explosion goes with a goal from the yellows
The ball, like fire, goes into the net
And a flow of cheers go off
An orange firework stops the match.

Miguel Bernabéu (9)
Archbishop Wake Primary School, Blandford

Happiness

Happiness is a football team
It is red as a cherry
It sounds like cheering
It smells like glory, glory.

Owen Hedicker (9)
Archbishop Wake Primary School, Blandford

Octopuses

Lucy reads
Quietly
Ella writes
Quickly
Elle thinks
Carefully
Bethan sits down
Calmly
Katie works
Happily
Tommy talks
Loudly
Bayley fiddles
Sneakily
Niko writes it down
Thoughtfully
Mohena copies down
Slowly
Lewis works hard
Skilfully.

Emily Park (8)
Archbishop Wake Primary School, Blandford

White Is . . .

A dreamy cloud
Gloomy polar bear
Soft Antarctic fox
Crunchy chalk
Smooth snow
Fluffy seals
Sweet sugar
Silk shirts
Rough cauliflowers.

Iona Caines (8)
Archbishop Wake Primary School, Blandford

The Storm

Lightning crashes, *bang!*
Wind blows, *whoosh!*
As the storm builds
The thunder gets wilder.
Crash! the rain explodes
With a howl of wind
Bursting into the sky.

Eruptions of wind,
Bangs of thunder,
Rumbling bolts of lightning
Come crashing and smashing
Through the sky.
A tsunami of water
Bursts out of the river.
With a rumbling meltdown
Things seem calm.

The weather seems calm
Krakatoa! The thunder howls
Lightning crashes
And rain floods the streets.

Liam Gonthier (10)
Archbishop Wake Primary School, Blandford

Octopuses

May was snoring *(zzzzz)*
Emily was hopping *(hop, hop)*
Aofia was yawning *(ah, ah)*
Ellie was sobbing *(waa)*
Bethan was hiding *(hee, hee)*
Olivia was shouting *(ahh)*
Lucy was acting *(I'm an actress)*
Ella was reading
Mrs Wakefield was writing
Miss Hensen was singing *(la, la)*.

Mohena Chowdhury (8)
Archbishop Wake Primary School, Blandford

My Acrostic School Poem

A ll children are chatting
R unning around the playground
C oming through the gates
H aving so much fun
B ecoming so good at everything
I t is so much fun when we have art
S chool has lots of different lessons
H opping around the classroom
O ctopuses is my class
P E is fun when we do athletics

W e all enjoy playtime
A t break time we all have fun
K icking footballs around
E veryone is enjoying themselves.

Lucy Brundish (8)
Archbishop Wake Primary School, Blandford

The Sea

Twirling, swirling, the sea is whirling,
It's waiting to dance,
Flooding, splashing, people get wet
Shining, blue, they have met the wet.
Flowers getting stronger
For they are getting weak
The people are amazed by the miracle
They don't dare go in,
But they just stare.
It is like an explosion you can never imagine.
When the sun comes up it will dry the wet
And then everybody will go back to normal.

Molly Blackwell (9)
Archbishop Wake Primary School, Blandford

Limericks

There was a young man called Pete
Who never stood on his feet
He walked on his hands
Which upset his glands
So then he sat in a seat!

There was a young boy called Paul
He liked to bounce this small ball
It fell on his head
So then he was dead
And his grave was very small!

There was a squirrel called Dave
Who stood on top of a cave
When the angels sang
Some guns went *bang, bang*
And Dave went down to his grave!

Bethan Amey (8)
Archbishop Wake Primary School, Blandford

The Football Match

As the match starts
The crowd are crashing through the entrance
Into their seats.
As Man U score the first goal
The away team
Explodes with joy.
The home team take a shot
Van der Sar is flowing through the air
And the home team bangs back
On their chairs.
The home team explodes with anger
Rooney takes a shot
Firing through the air.

Dan Spencer (10)
Archbishop Wake Primary School, Blandford

The Sea

The waves were as huge as a tall building
The cold water flowing over the rocks
The waves were as noisy as a supermarket
The blue sea was shining as bright as a colourful night sky
The flooded sand was as wet as a raining, grey day.

The mineral water was as clean as a cup full of sparkly water
The sparkling sea was as shiny as a blue diamond
The fishes swam into the current and hit the rocks.

The blue sea was as beautiful as a shimmering star
The freezing sea was as cold as a winter's morning

The lovely blue sea was as nice as any other sea
The wonderful sea suddenly stopped and it hit all of the rocks
                                        and it started again.

Emily Jones (9)
Archbishop Wake Primary School, Blandford

Fear

Fear is grey like gravel.
Fear sounds like the howl of a wolf.
Fear tastes like rotten eggs on a sunny day.
Fear smells like an angry skunk spraying like mad!
Fear looks like my PS2 being stolen!

Cameron Wellstead (9)
Archbishop Wake Primary School, Blandford

Silence

Silence reminds me of nice memories
It smells like the gentle smell of roses
It sounds like birds singing
It tastes of nothing
Silence feels like a gentle breeze.

Amy Phillips (9)
Archbishop Wake Primary School, Blandford

The Storm In The Middle Of The Sea

The sea was flowing nice and calm,
The wind was blowing gently,
You could feel the sea spitting on your arm,
So I meandered along the edge of the sea.

Suddenly, a storm grew,
You could hear the waves crashing against the rocks.
Houses were vibrating,
It sounded like the sky was erupting.

The wind was blowing in my face,
It was getting colder by the minute.
Babies were crying,
Then everything stopped!
And everyone stopped panicking.

Ruby Bircham (10)
Archbishop Wake Primary School, Blandford

The Rugby Match

We play the first match . . .
We are crashing up the field
Spetisbury score a smashing try
Blandford rush to score a try like a tsunami
Coach shouts like a hot potato.

Harun Cakir (10)
Archbishop Wake Primary School, Blandford

Limerick

There was a young girl from Peru
Who crashed into a truck full of glue.
She tried washing it off,
But it wouldn't come off,
So now she cannot eat her favourite stew.

Kai Williams (8)
Archbishop Wake Primary School, Blandford

School Time

S cience is so much fun
C lip art in ICT is so exciting
H omework is never handed in on time
O pportunities come every day
O vercoming test fears
L unchtime is second best at school

T elling people about stuff in 'show and tell'
I nside at break for being naughty
M usic is so much fun with Miss Henson
E verybody looks forward to home time!

Samuel Johnson (9)
Archbishop Wake Primary School, Blandford

Red Is . . .

A shiny cherry dangling from a stalk
A stunning robin's breast puffing and panting
Juicy strawberries lying in a box
A rosy apple hanging from a tree
A scarlet poppy blowing in the breeze
A pretty rose growing in the sun.

Katherine Stanley (7)
Archbishop Wake Primary School, Blandford

Blue Is . . .

Vicious sharks eating
Eyes staring
Chelsea tops and shorts
Berries, small, juicy and sweet
Clear, shiny sky
Reflecting, wavy sea.

Louie Ford (7)
Archbishop Wake Primary School, Blandford

The Sea

The waves were as high as a skyscraper
They were crashing against the rocks
The current was getting stronger and stronger
The water was invading the beach
Then there was a *big, gigantic* wave that flooded the beach
The sea became normal and calm again.

It started to rain
The sea was getting stronger again
The wind was howling as loud as a werewolf
Then *poof!* It suddenly stopped!

Lucy Park (10)
Archbishop Wake Primary School, Blandford

Red Is . . .

A roaring fire
An angry phoenix coming from the flames
A knobbly raspberry pecked by a blackbird
The motionless leaves hanging on the tree
The sunset slowly going down
A compacted fire extinguisher ready to pop
A light-reflecting ruby glimmering.

Ross Crabbe (9)
Archbishop Wake Primary School, Blandford

Brown Is . . .

Soft chocolate
A furry bear
A rough tree trunk
A crispy, dead leaf
A rock-hard conker
Flaky rust.

James Daly (8)
Archbishop Wake Primary School, Blandford

The Sea

The sea rumbles down the shore calmly,
Its clear, blue waters sparkle in the sunshine.
It bangs when it hits the hard brown rocks,
It feels like it would never erupt a tsunami.
The water doesn't flow, it races along the sand,
Then all of a sudden, the clear blue waters stop!
The water stayed like that for the rest of the night,
It looked as though a shark had struck a man,
It was just so quiet,
Then in the night the water suddenly turned dirty and murky.

Oliver Hooper (10)
Archbishop Wake Primary School, Blandford

The Giraffe

G obbling at leaves on trees
I am standing taller than one thousand bees
R unning through the strong wind
A ttacking from behind
F rantically I run away to hide
F eel the wind blowing in my face
E ndangered I am.

Sophie Babbs (10)
Archbishop Wake Primary School, Blandford

Green Is . . .

Lovely grass in a garden
Runny paint sliding off a table
Tasty apples, juicy to eat
Smooth stalks beneath flowers
Crunchy leaves under the trees
Prickly hedges, spiky to touch.

Dustin Gunning-Cole (8)
Archbishop Wake Primary School, Blandford

A Trip To The Supermarket

Bleep, bleep, bleep, goes the cash out,
A little child screams as the cash comes out.

Everywhere I could see there was metal flowing,
Trolleys, things I like are half-priced lollies.

Members of staff were all to see,
When I go there I always have a nice tea.

That is why I always shop at the market
Which is top!

Amy Lillywhite (9)
Archbishop Wake Primary School, Blandford

White Is . . .

The hard chalk
A delicate daisy's petals
Soft snow
Creased paper
A vicious polar bear
A clean shirt
A fluffy seal
Some long school socks.

Samantha Critchell (8)
Archbishop Wake Primary School, Blandford

Red Is . . .

A fire engine
A ripe apple
A robin's breast
A school sweatshirt
A ladybird's back
A lovely nose.

Tyler Lanes (8)
Archbishop Wake Primary School, Blandford

The Motorway

Traffic backed up for miles,
Looks like everyone will be stuck for a while.

A Vauxhall has caused a pile-up
By driving into an orange car.

The fire brigade arrives,
The police have to come
Or the chief will get an eyebrow pluck.

The ambulance fights through,
Wondering what on earth they have to do.

The families have babies
Which need changing.

The vibrations are like a tsunami,
Tearing an African village in two.

One car has ended up in the river,
Another has hit a milk truck.

Alex Cooper (10)
Archbishop Wake Primary School, Blandford

A Storm

Slowly the storm erupted,
The people were terrified.
It was getting colder by the second,
The houses and trees were vibrating,
People got into their shelters.

Dogs and cats got frightened
When the storm got worse.
The storm started lifting people's possessions.

Suddenly, the storm calmed down,
Then people stopped panicking
And were relieved.

Callum Goddard (10)
Archbishop Wake Primary School, Blandford

The Classroom

The classroom is empty after school,
Children learn there, short or tall,
And in each classroom,
Children's germs are others' tombs.
Day 1, day 2, day 3 and 4,
Pencils shorten more and more.
The end of term is finally here,
It's pretty late this time of year.
Vibrating floors bang as children explode into the room,
On toy day, someone had a broom.
It goes in a purplish ring,
The class pet is a tortoise that looks turtle (ish).

Connor Rosoman (10)
Archbishop Wake Primary School, Blandford

Green Is . . .

Sloppy green paint on a picture
Shiny leaves upon a tree
A slow tortoise crawling on the ground
A snapping crocodile chomping a fish
Inedible bananas hanging on a branch
Juicy broccoli on a plate
Crunchy lettuce full of water
A tweeting greenfinch in a tree.

Hannah Smith (8)
Archbishop Wake Primary School, Blandford

What's In The Box?

Beautiful diamonds shining like silver,
Yellow gold sparkling like the sun,
Red crystals glowing like fire,
Hundreds of tiny coins moving like water,
A black and white flag waving in the wind.

Fern Soda & Kamil Gradzewicz (10)
Archbishop Wake Primary School, Blandford

Motorway

Black, empty motorway
Then cars fire past
Spilling cars and lorries burn past
Road vibrating with speed
Wheels meltdown
Police flow down
Lorries crash in the flood
Drivers exploding
Old bangers steaming
Sports car melts the brakes.

Robert Newitt (10)
Archbishop Wake Primary School, Blandford

Happiness

Happiness is red
Happiness tastes like ice cream
Happiness sounds like the laughter of children
Happiness is fluffy like a cat
Happiness is like a hot summer's day.

Samuel Newman (9)
Archbishop Wake Primary School, Blandford

Red Is . . .

A juicy apple ripened in the sun
The fire extinguisher spreading gas
Fire, brighter than anything
Strawberries, sweeter than any I've seen
Poppies, silky and bright
Cherries, oh cherries, so small
Oh red paint, oh red paint so runny
The sky, oh light blue sky
Sunset, oh sunset, colourful sunset.

Lauren Newman (7)
Archbishop Wake Primary School, Blandford

The Street

The street is very busy, like an erupting volcano
Mums are chat, chat, chatting, they sound like the swans talking
There are lots of nice things in the shops, sparkling like a shiny river
The sun is shimmering like hot, yellow lava
People are rushing to work, like the river meandering
Lots of fast cars are as noisy as a volcano
The little children are making squeaky noises, like ducks quacking
At night the street is very dark, like the colour of a baby swan
The road is as dirty as a river in autumn.

Paige Smith (10)
Archbishop Wake Primary School, Blandford

Red Is . . .

The sweet cherries tasting so good
A sour raspberry that made me feel sick
The bright red Liverpool T-shirt blowing on a line
A juicy tomato, so juicy, the best
Delicious cranberries ready to pick
A heavy fire extinguisher blowing out a blazing fire.

Courtney McCormack (8)
Archbishop Wake Primary School, Blandford

Blue Is . . .

A clear sky in the morning
The crystal sea reflecting like a pearl
A ripe blueberry, sweet like a cherry
The flashing ambulance light in an emergency
Blue, squelchy paint drying in the light
A humungous, blue whale swimming in the sea
The blue, slithering snake wriggling around the jungle.

Holly Oliver (8)
Archbishop Wake Primary School, Blandford

The Motorway

There were cars rushing down the M25
I looked into the fields which were flooded with water
There was a *beep, beep*, Dad looked at the dashboard
There was no water in the radiator
Kaboom! The car steamed up
We opened the bonnet and called the RAC
I saw the flashing lights flowing down the motorway
The tired dogs were boiling up like a microwave
Mum put them on their leads
We let them out by the yellow, over-heated car
Mum was very upset about her Fiat Cinquecento Sport.

Mackenzie Reid (9)
Archbishop Wake Primary School, Blandford

Street Soccer

Loads of skills
As the crowd erupts
He flicks it high into the air
And catches it down
He does more skills
Till the bell and he leaves
The crowd goes wild
As he comes out
He does flicks and kicks
So fast in speed
The bell goes
His time's up
Everyone leaves.

Callum Wray (9)
Archbishop Wake Primary School, Blandford

What Would It Be Like . . .?

Falling out of a window
I see eating
I hear talking
I smell ice cream
I touch the windows
I taste cake.

Phebe Seaward (7)
Dover Park Primary School, Ryde

Jumping

G ood girl
E very day
O n the trampoline
R eally high like a
G iant
I n the garden
A ny time.

Georgia Watts (7)
Dover Park Primary School, Ryde

The Beach And Me!

R omans sailed to Britain
O n boats
M ost Romans were rich
A nd had money
N obody quit
S o they could save their family.

Lucy Grimbley (7)
Dover Park Primary School, Ryde

This Sweet World

Birdies flying and jumping little jumps
Running around and being chased
Drinking from the birdie bath
Jumping up the tree every day.

Trinity Magee (7)
Dover Park Primary School, Ryde

The Wrestler

Who feels cool?
Who needs money?
Who wants to win?
Who fears nothing?
Who would like a golden belt?

Jacob Rees (7)
Dover Park Primary School, Ryde

Traffic Jam

I see lots of cars
I hear horns
I smell gas
I touch the horn
I taste cake.

Scott Hemming (7)
Dover Park Primary School, Ryde

The White Lady

The white lady opens your front door
Goes up the creaking stairs
Turns your bedroom handle
But when the sun rises, she's gone!

Victoria McBoyle (9)
Grouville Primary School, Jersey

The Rock Monster

High up in the rocks lay a monster
Trembling, shivery and bald
Dressed in seaweed and barnacles
Alone and frightened in the cold.

Along came a boy, climbing the rocks
Slipping on the seaweed with his slippery socks
He startled the monster, who shrieked in delight
'Hello to you - you gave me a fright!'

Sophie Avant (7)
Grouville Primary School, Jersey

Through That Door

Through that door
Is a bubbling river
With blue water rushing down
And green, velvety moss
Sitting by its edge.
Through that door
Is a cornfield
Which rustles and rustles
In the wind.

Taryn Pontin (7)
Grouville Primary School, Jersey

My Grandad

My grandad is a green grape
A blue river that makes me giggle
He is a hard bed
My grandad is the sun
Shining across the hall
He is a bouncy ball.

Joni Gorman (7)
Grouville Primary School, Jersey

Shimmering Seaside

Glistening sea, bright as sapphires,
Covered with blurred reflections,
Like a smeared pastel picture on wrinkly, blue paper.
Golden sand stretched out for miles and miles,
Finally reaching a faraway sea.
In and out of rocky carpets,
Under and over shells and stones
And all the way back to me!
Tiny rock pools all around me,
Glowing tentacles swaying gently,
Crabs slipping from rock to rock quickly and carefully
With their red eyes.
Starfish clinging onto rocks with patterns,
So hard to see.
I wonder, tomorrow what I'm going to see.

Josephine Carnegie (7)
Grouville Primary School, Jersey

What Would I Do?

What would I do
If I was a shoe?

If I only knew that
I was a brown, old shoe!

Would I sing or play
Or stay at home all day?

I really don't know
What I would do

What would *you* do
If it was you?

Cerian Mason (8)
Grouville Primary School, Jersey

Elvis

Elvis
Ran around the garden
Looking like a carrot
With legs.
Now
Elvis can't
Splash me
Squeak at me
Or
Munch his
Food.
Elvis
My guinea pig
Is gone.
Emma Wildbore-Hands (9)
Grouville Primary School, Jersey

Caterpillar

Caterpillar
On
My
Finger
Tickling
As he
Crawls
His hairy legs
Moving
Slowly
I giggle
When he goes.
Isobel Kelly (8)
Grouville Primary School, Jersey

Volcano

Volcano erupts
Oozing lava
Burning heat
Mud flows
Thick sludge
Black ash
Blocks out the light.

Carys Ingram (9)
Grouville Primary School, Jersey

My Mum

My mum is a grape
A purple whoopee cushion
That makes me embarrassed.
She is a bouncy castle
A flowing stream.
My mum is the bright sun.
She is a mad doll
Giggling and laughing.

Amber Smith (10)
Grouville Primary School, Jersey

My Hamster

My hamster is
A fluffy warm blanket
With
Two shiny
Black eyes
An electric body
With a
Warm
Loving
Heart.

Uma Le Boutillier (8)
Grouville Primary School, Jersey

Through That Door

Through that door
Is an erupting volcano
Gushing out candy.

Through that door
Is a wicked witch
Who never stops laughing.

Through that door
Is a scaly, pink dragon
Blowing out blue fire.

Erin & Neve Lynch (8)
Grouville Primary School, Jersey

The Magic Box
(Based on 'Magic Box' by Kit Wright)

I will put in my box . . .

The tiniest best whiteboard
A fabulous flying fog
A million pound electric pen

I will put in my box . . .

A dog miaowing and a cat barking
An elephant with a short nose and a man with a long nose
A plate that's blown up and a ball that's flat

I will put in my box . . .

The smell of a chicken just cooked
The touch of a newborn kitten
Hearing the bacon sizzling in the oven

My box will be made from Chocolate Buttons
And mint ice cream that shines in the light
In my box I will play at the beach and park.

Amber Cheverton (9)
Mill Rythe Junior School, Hayling Island

My Magic Box
(Based on 'Magic Box' by Kit Wright)

I will put in my box . . .
The excitement of an amazing roller coaster,
A picture of people I saw in a dream,
A heated pool of the bluest water.

I will put in my box . . .

The smell of fresh, juicy strawberries,
A winter's day with snow on the ground ready to throw,
The glimpse of the sun for the first time, yellow as sand.

I will put in my box . . .

The first tree growing,
An alien living on Earth,
A man living on Mars.

I will put in my box . . .

An amazing myth coming true,
The green trees in spring,
A memory of my family.

My magic box is fashioned
From the purest gold in the world,
From sparkling, gleaming silver,
The corners are the bones of ancient dinosaurs.

I get in my box.
It's a dream come true.
I have the smell of strawberries,
Snow on the floor,
A myth come true,
A yellow sun,
Green trees
And my family everywhere.

I will take this box to the farthest corner of the world
To see starving children.
I will show them my box
And they will laugh and smile.

Jamie Maddison (9)
Mill Rythe Junior School, Hayling Island

My Mysterious Box
(Based on 'Magic Box' by Kit Wright)

I will put in my box . . .

Mysterious memories from dreams long gone,
A special secret from a spectacular friend,
The final gleaming smile from my mum and dad.

I will put in my box . . .

The stride of a devil,
Everlasting frost from a magical snowman,
A lucky spark from a spooky spider.

I will put in my box . . .

A diamond as precious as the Queen's jewels,
The gold and treasure from a pirate's galleon,
A mouse eating a carrot and a rabbit eating cheese.

I will put in my box . . .

A smile of a baby girl,
The swishing breeze of a silky summer day,
The sun as cold as ice and the sun as hot as fire.

I will put in my box . . .

A loveable lamp full of light,
A ball bouncing as high as the sky,
The pitter-patter of the rain pelting down.

My box is fashioned in gold.
Its hinges are made out of lollipops.
The handle is made out of bananas.
My box is as soft as cotton wool.

I shall go to Egypt in my box,
On the great, high sculptures made out of marble and clay
And look at the beautiful views of the pyramids.

Georgia Rix (9)
Mill Rythe Junior School, Hayling Island

The Magic Box
(Based on 'Magic Box' by Kit Wright)

I will put in my box . . .

The paw of a little tiger cub,
The swish of a slithering snake
And the birthstone of a dragon.

I will put in my box . . .

The sparkle from a shiny sea horse,
A penguin from the snowiness of Antarctica
And a young starfish from an old rock pool.

I will put in my box . . .

A flame from the sun,
A piece of rock from the moon
And some toxic gas from Neptune.

I will put in my box . . .

A bowl of sparkling fruit,
An orange apple
And a green carrot.

I will put in my box . . .

The juice of a zingy blackcurrant,
The root of an ancient wishing tree
And the last squeak of a sparkly, white mouse.

I will put in my box . . .

A single dewdrop in the garden,
A petal from the only rose
And a feather from a flying finch.

My box is fashioned from
Clear, purple crystals of ice and glass,
With the moon on the lid
And gems from far away in the corners.
The lock is a gnarled finger of an ancient ancestor.

It will take me to the lost world of Atlantis,
On a crystal boat,
To the last place I'd want to be.

Georgina Mill (9)
Mill Rythe Junior School, Hayling Island

Magic Box
(Based on 'Magic Box' by Kit Wright)

I will put in the box . . .

Millions of mega money
A big, bold, brilliant book
My friends Jake and Travis

I will put in the box . . .

A fabulous, fantastic football
I can hear it bouncing on the ground
And a holiday on the moon

I will put in the box . . .

A piece of cake from a birthday
A fang from a vampire
And a decoration from a Christmas tree

My box is crafted from silver
The hinges are skeleton bones
And it has a black hole inside it

I will put my box under my bed
With all my other special things
And every day I will take it out
And look at the amazing sight.

Joseph Drayton (9)
Mill Rythe Junior School, Hayling Island

Magic Box
(Based on 'Magic Box' by Kit Wright)

I will put in my box . . .

A swishy, swashy puppy dog tail,
The final memory of my loving grandpa,
A cheeky, brown, baby monkey from the deepest jungle.

I will put in my box . . .

The sweet, tropical tang of a grapefruit,
A fluffy, black penguin from the North Atlantic islands,
Pictures of the foreign lands I have travelled to.

I will put in my box . . .

The first snowflake falling from a dark, moody sky,
A silver fish, bright as the sun,
A dewdrop from a spider's web on a frosty morning.

I will put in my box . . .

A boo from a ghost on Hallowe'en,
A noisy sniff from a winter cold,
The brightest twinkle from a dazzling star.

I will put in my box . . .

A blue banana and a purple pumpkin,
A clucking cow and a mooing hen,
The thick, woolly hair from a squeaking pig.

My box is fashioned from bubbles and ice,
With yellow suns on the corners
And the shiny moon on the lid.
Its hinges are made with fat branches
From the tallest tree.

I shall fly in my box,
In the sunset sky of Africa,
Then land in my bed in a bundle of giggles,
Wrapped up in my mother's arms.

Megan Capaldi-Tallon (9)
Mill Rythe Junior School, Hayling Island

Magic Box
(Based on 'Magic Box' by Kit Wright)

I will put in my box . . .

A picture of my old hamster, never to be forgotten,
A clear, blue, swishing waterfall
Fringed by lush, tropical plants,
My precious birthstone that means the world.

I will put in my box . . .

A single red rose with prickly thorns,
The glow of the sinking sun
And one everlasting, enchanting snowflake.

I will put in my box . . .

A mooing pig,
An oinking cow,
A tub of glittery wishes.

I will put in my box . . .

A pot of bubbles,
A piece of faded paper with my first scribble,
A penguin on a block of ice.

I will put in my box . . .

A princess with a crown,
A parrot from the rainforest,
A castle from a never forgotten dream
And my all so important family.

My box is fashioned from . . .

Clear sea glass from the bottomless, deep, dark waters
And diamonds and jewels from the deepest mine.

I shall ride on my surfboard down the waterfall
With the wind in my hair
And land in my soft bed
And dream sweet dreams of being far, far away.

Emily Richardson (10)
Mill Rythe Junior School, Hayling Island

My Magic Box
(Based on 'Magic Box' by Kit Wright)

I will put in my box . . .

The first flicker of fire on Earth,
A shining icicle from another world,
The crunching of leaves in the cold wind.

I will put in my box . . .

A bucket of the coldest water from the Atlantic Ocean,
All of the soft, sandy, yellow beaches from Spain
And the twinkling, beautiful stars in space.

I will put in my box . . .

Photos of special family and friends
And a happy Mum and Dad,
Special thoughts of whispering wishes.

I will put in my box . . .

A 25th hour and a 13th month,
A huge fire-breathing dog
And a gentle, humble dragon.

My box is made from diamonds and steel,
Its lid is an ancient coffin,
Its colours are red and blue
And its hinges are solid gold.

I will dance in my box,
On the spotless, crystal diamond floor,
Of a magical house,
Made with glistening glass.

Francesca Ramsbottom (9)
Mill Rythe Junior School, Hayling Island

My Secret Box
(Based on 'Magic Box' by Kit Wright)

I will put in my box . . .

A twinkling torch as bright as the stars,
A bowl of spaghetti slouching in my mouth,
A poster posted by a postman.

I will put in my box . . .

The smell of a dirty baby,
The touch of a furry dog,
The taste of a licked lolly,
The miaow of a curious cat that you can hear,
The sight of a wobbly wall.

I will put in my box . . .

Faded photos from the past,
The memories of seeing my gran,
The memories of me at a primary school.

I will put in my box . . .
A witch in an army tank,
An army man on a broomstick.

My box is fashioned from bronze, copper and steel
With diamonds on the lid and friends in the corners.
Its hinges are the finger joints of humans.

I will live in my box
Near the high-flying fish in the Atlantic,
With friends and family at my side.

I will keep my box hidden forever,
So no one will touch or come near it.
My box will remain hidden.

David Lasham (9)
Mill Rythe Junior School, Hayling Island

Magic Box
(Based on 'Magic Box' by Kit Wright)

I will put in the box . . .

A CD of Paulo Nutini to remind me of Scotland
And calm me down.
Photos of my fabulous, fun friends and family.
A sample of the finest ice-cold Fanta
And the memories of my marvellous and mysterious life.

I will put in the box . . .

A fish being kicked into a goal
And a football swimming in a tank.
A plain beach with tall palm trees
And tropical fish in the waters.
A fishing rod to remind me of my many fishing trips
My dad and I went on.
A piece of glinting, glamorous gold to lighten my day.

I will put in the box . . .

A quad bike on a trampoline playing airoball
And a football on a dirt course.

My box has a lock of pure diamond
And the hinges are of hard chocolate.
Its surface is made of melted gold and silver in a mottled design.

I shall skateboard in my box
And be cast upon a big field of long grass.

Euan Condron (9)
Mill Rythe Junior School, Hayling Island

The Magic Box
(Based on 'Magic Box' by Kit Wright)

I will put in my box . . .

Some cold, creamy caramel ice cream,
The whitest, icy snow from Mount Fuji
And the scary, spooky skeletons and monsters' celebration
                                            of Hallowe'en.

I will put in my box . . .

A bar of Cadbury's chocolate oozing with Cream Egg,
A squeaky, noisy, fat guinea pig
And a dazzling, shiny diamond.

I will put in my box . . .

Fading photos of my fabulous family,
The first glimpse of my small, smiley baby sister
And some golden sand from my heavenly holidays.

I will put in my box . . .

An 8th day and a pink moon,
A pony that swims in the ocean
And a dolphin that canters around its field.

My box is fashioned from silver, paper and gold
With mysteries in the corners and music on the lid.

I will travel the world with the box under my arm,
The answer to every question is in my box.

Libby Dunaway (9)
Mill Rythe Junior School, Hayling Island

The Magic Box
(Based on 'Magic Box' by Kit Wright)

I will put in my box . . .

Family diamonds that dazzle in the dancing sun,
Photos of a precious and lost family,
Marvellous memories of miraculous moments.

I will put in my box . . .

The smell of my mum making dinner,
The soft touch of Heidi's iced buns,
The sound of the waves crashing against the beach.

I will put in my box . . .

The first smile of my sister,
The first glimpse of my new house,
The first cuddle with my mum.

I will put in my box . . .

A dolphin in a web,
A spider in the sea,
A snowman with an ice cream.

My box is covered with Egyptian cloth,
It has a heart-shaped lock,
It is engraved with ancient hieroglyphics.

I can do anything in my box,
It is my very special place where all my dreams can come true.
There is no limit to what I can imagine in my box.

Georgia Tame (9)
Mill Rythe Junior School, Hayling Island

The Magic Box
(Based on 'Magic Box' by Kit Wright)

I will put in the box . . .

The sun as a shimmering, shiny sight of light
The moon as a silver ball in the sky
The stars on a dark night

I will put in the box . . .

The soft fur of a dog
The noise of a snake hissing
The sight of a teddy bear walking

I will put in the box . . .

A bunny nibbling on a carrot
A wish from my great nan
A dog digging a hole

I will put in the box . . .

A tortoise that is so fast
And a cheetah that is so slow
A cat that can fly

My box is made out of glass
And a magic rainbow
With stars in the corner
And the hinges of angels' wings

I will fly in my box
To a different world where no one knows me
To see the moon and the flowers from the sun.

Bryony Brennan (9)
Mill Rythe Junior School, Hayling Island

The Magic Box
(Based on 'Magic Box' by Kit Wright)

I will put in my box . . .

A puppy playing and pouncing around,
A special scent of a favourite flower,
A swish of the silent, swaying wind.

I will put in my box . . .

A dolphin diving, dazzling and dancing,
The taste of milky chocolate,
The glitter of the twinkling stars.

I will put in my box . . .

The bang of a booming, beautiful firework,
The first time I walked by myself,
A picture of my family and friends.

I will put in my box . . .

One new planet with life on it,
Tea in a plant pot,
A rose in a mug.

I will put in my box . . .

The sea as blue as topaz,
An apple as red as a ruby,
A tulip as purple as amethyst.

My box is made of . . .

A special 40,000-year-old tree called the Kauri tree,
With hinges made out of sparkling diamonds
And pink flowers, hearts and stars on the edges of the box.

I would use my box by . . .

Cherishing it forever,
When I click my fingers,
There it would be, as good as new.

Chloe Bethell (10)
Mill Rythe Junior School, Hayling Island

The Magic Box
(Based on 'Magic Box' by Kit Wright)

I will put in the box . . .

Marvellous music that's heard all around
Flickering fish finding their fins
Silly, skinny, singing clowns

I will put in the box . . .

A man's big laugh
The sound of a bird's wing
The biggest waterfall ever

I will put in the box . . .

The sea's splashing, crashing waves
A cat in the wind
A baby playing football
And a man sucking his thumb

I will put in the box . . .

The first step of a baby child
A child's special secrets
A lion hopping around
And a rabbit running on four legs

I will put in the box . . .

A life living dream
The whitest cloud in the sky
A flash of lightning in the sky

My box will be fashioned
With leather and crocodile skin
With its toes in the corners

I shall go in my box
And lie on the greenest grass
Then discover the memories from the past.

Jake Todd (9)
Mill Rythe Junior School, Hayling Island

My Box
(Based on 'Magic Box' by Kit Wright)

I will put in my box . . .

A pig in a bath,
A human in a pigsty,
A snow globe from my grandad.

I will put in my box . . .

A crack from a firework,
My favourite pair of shoes
And my first toy.

I will put in my box . . .

A spider from Hallowe'en,
A priceless diamond with a twinkle in the centre
And the miaow of a cat.

I will put in my box . . .

A flickering flaming firework,
A secret from a friend
And a first smile of a baby.

My box is fashioned with . . .

Spiral patterns on the lid
And is made from chocolate.
The hinges are made from dark chocolate.

I will swim in my box
In the Indian Ocean,
Where nobody has been.

Selena Williams (9)
Mill Rythe Junior School, Hayling Island

The Magic Box
(Based on 'Magic Box' by Kit Wright)

I will put in the box . . .

A panther as black as coal
A mole that lives in a hole
A teddy bear all soft and cuddly

I will put in the box . . .

A diamond carved in the face of a tiger
A galloping horse
And a wooden chair made from an ancient oak tree

I will put in the box . . .

A slippery snake slithering through the jungle
A terrific trampoline
And a big, blue balloon

I will put in the box . . .

The eighth day of the week
A woolly scarf made from the finest wool
And Christmas

My box has hinges made from dragon's claws
And is made of gold
It has wishes in the corners

It is the most precious thing I have
And I will treasure it forever.

Jessica Easton (9)
Mill Rythe Junior School, Hayling Island

The Magic Box
(Based on 'Magic Box' by Kit Wright)

I will put in my box . . .

A solar system so happy and bright
A bouncy basketball on my bedroom floor
A small, dainty daisy

I will put in my box . . .

A bass guitar being plucked away
The smell of shampoo bouncing around my face
The wind rustling through the trees

I will put in my box . . .

My first ever meal of taste and splendour
An adventure with a fire-breathing polar bear
A dragon eating ice

I will put in my box . . .

A dead night, spooky and black
A top on a tarantula with a twinkle in the thigh
A scarlet secret from a little girl

I will put in my box . . .

A star from the southern sky
And see it shine forever

The fashion of my box will be . . .

Made of chocolate, smooth and delicious
There will be hinges of flower stems green and bright
The inside will gleam with a reflection of white chocolate

I will run in my box . . .

I will start on green grass
And end on colourful gravel
And think of my journey through life.

Mia Wick (9)
Mill Rythe Junior School, Hayling Island

Countdown Animals

I dreamt 10 snakes came slithering by,
But I was shy, they would go in my eye.

I dreamt 9 snakes came slithering by,
I thought they came to say hi.

I dreamt 8 dogs came barking by,
Four tried to say hi, the others started to cry.

I dreamt 7 dogs came barking by,
They thought there were dogs in the sky.

I dreamt 6 parrots were squawking in their cage,
Six parrots were eating their carrots.

I dreamt 5 parrots were squawking in their cage,
Four were polite, but one got a fright.

I dreamt 4 spiders came scurrying by
And they tried to say goodbye.

I dreamt 3 spiders came scurrying by,
Two of them jumped up high.

I dreamt 2 tigers came roaring by,
And they ate a spider who was playing 'I Spy'.

I dreamt of all the animals coming by,
They all said goodbye.

Kieran McHardy & Charlie Rogers (8)
Portway Junior School, Andover

My Horse

Turns into fire
His muscles and his bones
His breath is the fire
Blowing in my skin
His hooves are shining stones
His mane and tail are flickering flames
As red as gleaming embers.

Mehgan Skelton (7)
Portway Junior School, Andover

The Purrfect Fire

My cat turns into fire
His muscles and his bones
His breath is flying sparks like a young dragon's fire
His eyes are the orange heat
His tail and legs are lots of ash as black as charcoal
And we never knew what happened since my cat went up in flames.

Georgia Day (7)
Portway Junior School, Andover

I Dream Of Monkey Magic

My monkey turns into fire
His muscles and his bones
His breath is flickering fire
His teeth are boiling hot
His skin and hair are roaring fire
As hot as if you touched the sun.

Harry Smallbones (7)
Portway Junior School, Andover

Moonlight Bright

In the moonlight shining bright
Wolves howl in the night.

The night is dark, you can't see
You don't know if he is watching you.

Watch the shadows bright at night
It may give you a big fright.

Next time you know it
You're in your bed
Don't forget it's in your head.

Connor McMullen & Lewis Coggins (9)
Portway Junior School, Andover

In My Dream I Saw The Tallest Tower

I saw a flower of the finest kind,
I saw a man with super powers,
I saw my mum, she is so dumb,
I saw a boy do a sum,
I saw a light, it was so bright,
I saw a dog fight with all its might,
I saw a horse, it was badly injured,
I saw some sauce in a jar,
I saw a wolf howl in the darkest hour,
I saw all this in the tallest tower.

Luke Jackson (8)
Portway Junior School, Andover

The Fire Dog

My brown dog turns into some orange fire
His muscles and his bones
His breath is hot fire flickering above the trees
His head is coal
His tail and legs are fireworks
As yellow as fire bombs.

Kingsley Pannell (7)
Portway Junior School, Andover

My Fire Penguin

My penguin turns into fire
His muscles and his bones
His breath is the light of a bonfire
His beak is as light as the sun
His belly and back are as black as ashes
As bright as sparks on the fire.

Nathan Birks (7)
Portway Junior School, Andover

The Dream

I had a dream next Monday week
Beneath the apple trees
I saw a cat eat a bat
And a dog sat in a bog.
I dreamed I saw a frog in the fog,
How weird was that?
And saw a lizard that drank fizzy drink
Then his mouth went pink
And a rabbit was at my door.
I dreamt I saw my hamster eat all my washing,
It got very fat
After that!
I saw a dolphin swirling round
In a little pearl,
I thought it was a fish,
So I ate it up,
It made me want to throw up.
I dreamt I saw a monkey,
Acting all funky.

Chloe Brookes (9) & Lizzie White (8)
Portway Junior School, Andover

I Dreamt A Dream

I dreamt a dream I can't remember
I dreamt a dream of November
I dreamt a dream in my head
I dreamt a dream on my bed
I dreamt a dream in a car
I dreamt a dream driving far
I dreamt a dream about a bird
Where something strange occurred
I dream this dream every night
I dreamt in this dream I had a fright.

Jordan Day (8) & Alex Morling (9)
Portway Junior School, Andover

The Dragon In A Wagon

I once had a magical dream,
I was walking past a flowing stream.
I tiptoed past a dark cave,
I was very brave.
So I reluctantly went in,
Thinking it was used like a bin.
When I came out the side,
It was a land where creatures did collide,
But there was a boneshaking roar
And I turned and saw,
A friendly looking green dragon,
Stuck in a little brown wagon.
He was roaring in pain,
I helped him in vain.
He struggled and wiggled about,
While I pulled him out.
He thanked me nice
And ate some mice.
So I invited him over,
Back to Andover.
He disappeared by the stream,
I woke up, just a dream.
Or was it?

Alice Bathie & Kayleigh Morris (8)
Portway Junior School, Andover

I Dreamt

I dreamt a dog was eating a bone
I dreamt a dog was quite alone
I dreamt a dog was in mid-air
I dreamt of a dog eating nuts
I dreamt of a dog with a bleeding cut
I dreamt of my nan's dog because it died
I dreamt of the dog
And I woke up and cried.

Dana Shelley (9) & Gabrielle Snook (8)
Portway Junior School, Andover

Dreaming

She dreamt of a cupboard with a gloomy, murky toy box quite long,
The colours were pink and red.
The lid lifted slowly,
She turned for the door but then heard footsteps.

She turned round quickly
To find toys walking towards her with faces very long.

She ran to her mum's room, but no one was there,
So she ran to the door when suddenly she woke
And realised that nothing had happened.
It was all a dream, but she was still shivering with fear.

Tayla Moody (8)
Portway Junior School, Andover

Attack Of Ground Crack

It was a dreadful sight to see,
Not in the sky,
Not on the land,
Nowhere!
Nothing . . .
A giant crack approached
    Down
        They
            All
                Fell
Except one.
It was dark.
It was a nightmare!

Luke Holden (8)
Portway Junior School, Andover

The Dying Land

I dreamt of a land that was dying,
Everything was dark and grey.
Animals were getting slow because of the silence,
Colour wasn't in anything, not even in the sky.

I dreamt of a land where plants wouldn't grow,
Everything was still,
Colour wasn't in anything, not even in the sky.

I dreamt of a land that was drowning in the rivers and the seas,
Colour wasn't in anything, not even in the sky.

Siân Allen (9)
Portway Junior School, Andover

Sweetland The One

What did you dream about?
I dreamt about a land called Sweetland.
It was full of sweets and chocolate rivers.
What was it like?
It was really, really fun.
I liked it a lot.
Did you eat anything?
Yes, of course I did.
I ate sweets, chocolate rivers
And candyfloss.
Did you want to stay there?
Yes, I did want to stay there.
I wish my dream would come true.

Cerys Revelle-Scully & Cassie Shearer (8)
Portway Junior School, Andover

Minibeasts' Battle

I dreamt there were three little caterpillars on a leaf,
I dreamt there were three spiders on the leaf and I scared
                                        them away.
I dreamt the three caterpillars crawled away.
I dreamt there were three spiders on a leaf eating lunch.
I dreamt there were two little ants on the leaf, showing their
                                        sharp teeth.
I dreamt the three spiders crawled away.
I dreamt there were two little ants on the leaf eating their lunch
                                        in the thin air.

Jing-Ying Wong & Courtney Tobin (8)
Portway Junior School, Andover

My Special Holiday Dream

I had a dream,
I had a dream I was on a brilliant holiday.
I had a dream I was on a wonderful sandy beach.
I had a dream I was swimming in the beautiful, warm ocean.
I had a dream I was sunbathing in the lovely, hot sun.
I had a dream, I had a very special dream.

Amber Casselton (8)
Portway Junior School, Andover

My Snow Deer

My deer turns into snow
His breath is a whirlwind whooshing through the trees
His eyes are balls of snow
His ears and his head are snowflakes
Then he turns into blocks of snow.

Britney Enright (7)
Portway Junior School, Andover

Seascape

S eagulls squawking, swiftly soaring through the baby-blue sky
E veryone eating lunch like little mice nibbling
A bout the rock pools the crispy crab scuttles through the seaweed
S hips sail on the whisky white horses jumping over and over
C atfish flap through the mouldy, colourful coral
A nimals so little that you can hardly see them
P eople gathering all their things together
E ating delicious soft ice cream for the last time.

Scott Gallichan (10)
St John's School, Jersey

My Seascape Poem

S ea crashing on the rocky, mouldy wall
E lectric eels swimming around the salty sea
A ll kinds of disgusting rubbish lying on the shoreline
S melly debris surrounding freshly built sandcastles
C astles of sand being stomped upon
A cross the sandy beach parents call their children
P eople investigating rock pool habitats
E vening breaks and emptiness descends on the beach.

Bryce Leatt (10)
St John's School, Jersey

Seascape

S ea crashing and clashing down on rocks
E choing and producing everlasting cracks on the sea
A lighting the sea, is the bright reflection of the moon
S cavenging birds fight for food
C aves have water silently lurking into them
A gentle moon shimmers like a diamond
P eople collecting pollution and putting it into bags
E vening comes as the day has gone.

Verity Stanier (10)
St John's School, Jersey

My Seascape Poem

S eagulls are squawking and swooping, anticipating interesting food
E veryone is eating quietly on the beach like little mice munching and crunching
A round the rock pool, crabs scuttle looking for a safe environment
S hipwrecks have been explored by explorers, their stories waiting to be told
C atfish search for food in the night
A nimals dig for cover in the sapphire light
P eople are swimming in the salty, fish-infested sea
E dible food is being eaten by scavenging animals.

Kealan Bisson (10)
St John's School, Jersey

Seascape Poem

S ea crashes against the rocks
E rosion causes tiny grains of rock to make the golden sand
A taste of salt from the sea touches my lips
S and looks like rocks that have been crushed into 1 million pieces
C oming down from nowhere, the darkness falls
A bove the people, morning lies above them
P eople swimming in the salty sea and fish darting in and out
E ating ice cream on the beach.

Ryan Hillion (10)
St John's School, Jersey

I Like . . .

I like the taste of juicy apples crunching in my mouth
I like the smell of salty roast potatoes rippling up my nose
I like the feel of fluffy feathers tickling my hands
I like the sound of golden bells echoing in my ears
I like the sight of flashing fireworks sparkling in my eyes.

Jessica Slack (7)
St John's School, Jersey

My Seascape Poem

S ea booming against the crumbling rock face
E veryone packing up quickly to race home
A light with streetlights as the sun floods behind the sloping hill
S crambling down an echoing cave as the ocean plunges into the
    once again lively rock pools
C hilling breezes sweep around me as I stroll with my bouncy dog
A lonely figure stands out near the sea, singing quietly
P eople at the top of the beach watch the crashing waves
E veryone is rushing to pack away as the rolling waves creep
    up the beach.

Niamh Whiteman (10)
St John's School, Jersey

Seascape Poem

S eaweed washed up on the brim of the sea's shoreline like a
    swivelling snake
E vening skies bring scorching hot barbecues
A gainst the dull, grey walls, a sight of splattered ice creams
S himmering moonlit sea brings a moment of peace and relaxation
C rashing waves like a thundery storm
A seagull screeching for food like a fire alarm
P eople making grand sandcastles on the chilly sand
E normous waves chase away boisterous young children.

Luna Pinto Baker (11)
St John's School, Jersey

I Like . . .

I like the taste of sweets melting in my mouth
I like the feel of the rain falling on my face
I like the sound of birds whistling in the trees
I like the smell of popcorn drifting up my nose
I like the sight of the computer flashing at my eyes.

Alice Mitchell (7)
St John's School, Jersey

Seascape

S eabirds are gliding and swooping down over the dark blue sea
E veryone is busy enjoying the gleaming sun and the golden,
sandy beach
A nd over by the galleys, the choppy sea crashes wildly against
the rough, craggy rocks
S urfers continue to glide and skim with the waves across the bay
C hildren scrambling with excitement and their nets amongst the
rock pools
A dults lying down toasting in the gleaming, hot sun
P eople are walking their dogs all around the gleaming beach
E nd of a glorious, relaxing day and everyone is going home feeling
happy, tired, hungry and ready for bed and a new day tomorrow.

Ashton Breen-Faudemer (10)
St John's School, Jersey

Seascape

S eagulls scavenging for leftovers on the beach
E verlasting waves crashing against the sand
A dog whizzes across the sparkling sand
S hrimps dart across the water like shooting stars in the sky
C aves light up as the blazing sun arrives
A ll around smelly, slimy seaweed fills the beach
P eople start to come to the beach in their loud, humming cars
E verything starts to get ready for a fantastic new day.

Jack Dorey (10)
St John's School, Jersey

I Like . . .

I like the taste of white chocolate melting in my mouth
I like the smell of hot fire sizzling up my nose
I like the feel of soft cats tickling my hands
I like the sound of gentle wind flashing in my ears
I like the sight of children playing, dashing side to side.

Bradley Cox (7)
St John's School, Jersey

Seascape

S ea glistening like emeralds in an unnatural light
E verybody going to the sunny seaside
A nother fog horn from a foul-smelling fishing boat
S eagulls frantically swooping to catch fish
C rustaceans scurry to cover under crusty seaweed
A plate of fish and chips fried in boiling oil
P eople clambering along jagged rocks and swimming in the sea
                                                                          as flat as a pond
E vening rids the beach of visitors like a cat scatters birds from
                                                                                    a tree.

Christopher Beynon (10)
St John's School, Jersey

Seascape Poem

S ea crashes against the hard, spiky rocks
E xcited children leap into the cold, stormy sea
A ll sorts of shoe prints embedded in the sand
S alty sea spray splashes into the air and onto my lips
C lams being washed up onto the beach by violent oceans
A cross the light, fluffy beaches, parents play catch with
                                                                          their children
P eople practising for various walks
E very boat exits the harbour to enjoy the serenity of a summer's day.

Harry Lewis (10)
St John's School, Jersey

I Like . . .

I like the taste of yummy lemon sweets sizzling on my tongue
I like the smell of burning electricity flying up my nostrils
I like the feel of my very soft teddy on my hand
I like the sound of my very loud cat miaowing in my ears
I like the sight of a colourful hot air balloon.

Jamie Stewart (7)
St John's School, Jersey

Seascape

S ea battering against the cold, stark rocks,
E ngraving dents and cracks in the rugged wall.
A bove in the sky, seagulls scavenging for bread and discarded food.
S ailing boats going out to sea to find sea creatures,
C hasing fish as they dart across the water, as the sea makes a
　　　　　　　　　　　　　　　　　　　　　　　loud crashing noise.
A wful, disgusting moss climbing up the bumpy wall.
P eople relaxing and having a wonderful time at the beach.
E veryone leaving, as the scorching sun goes down.

Jacob Allix (10)
St John's School, Jersey

I Like . . .

I like the taste of hot Chinese food spicing in my mouth
I like the smell of roast beef dinner burning up my nose
I like the feel of soft, red velvet tickling my hands
I like the sound of Santa's golden bells dinging on his
　　　　　　　　　　　　　　　　　　Christmas sleigh
I like the sight of my dog and I walking with my dad on the cliff path
　　　　　　　　　　　　　　　　　　　　　　　at Devil's Hole.

Sadie Pinnock (7)
St John's School, Jersey

I Like . . .

I like the taste of sweet honey dribbling in my mouth
I like the smell of lovely flowers shooting up my nostrils
I like the feel of my cute dog cuddling up to me
I like the sound of hard stones plopping in the water
I like the sight of small birds flying in the air.

Shaynee Whiteman (7)
St John's School, Jersey

If I Were A Devil . . .

I'd burn 1,000 houses and quietly run as fast as the wind
And I would crush people's hope as I go.
I would fly quickly through the air like a dragon looking for its prey.
People would scream wildly.
The fire of 100,000 bodies could not destroy me.
I would have my one magic island without anybody knowing
And burn 100 forests.
I would be very, very lonely, but I would have to find a friend
Sooner or later.
I would have Mum, Dad and Felicity to look after me.

If only I were a devil.

Magdalena Thébault (8)
St John's School, Jersey

If I Were A Ghost . . .

If I were a ghost . . .

I'd fly around and look at the people beyond the ground.
I'd wait until I could fly into people's houses and then *boom!*
Crash loudly into the window.
I'd sleep in a wave and crash into people's graves.

If only I were a ghost!

Khaya Pybus (8)
St John's School, Jersey

I Like . . .

I like the taste of hard sweets crunching on my teeth
I like the sound of big drums beating in my ear
I like the smell of hot gravy sliding up my nose
I like the feel of wet rain dripping down my face
I like the sight of beautiful stars sparkling in my eyes.

Ellie Cooper (7)
St John's School, Jersey

If Only I Was A Griffin

If only I was a griffin . . .
I would sprint my fiery powers to unlock chambers,
Get out and dash, then sprint.
I would stride quickly and quietly.
I am a fierce griffin.
I don't like people.
I scare people fiercely with my vicious voice.

If only I was a griffin!

Sam Masefield (8)
St John's School, Jersey

I Like . . .

I like the taste of hot, spicy pepperoni burning on my tongue
I like the smell of chocolate ice cream wafting up my nose
I like the feel of a cold ice pack freezing on my face
I like the sound of loud music clashing in my ears
I like the sight of the big Eiffel Tower flashing in the night.

Leon Couriard (7)
St John's School, Jersey

I Like . . .

I like the taste of hot, spicy pasta burning on my tongue
I like the smell of tasty spaghetti zooming up my nose
I like the feel of blue play dough, gooey in my hands
I like the sound of noisy people chatting really, really loudly
I like the light of bright colours flashing on the computer screen.

Frankie Jones (7)
St John's School, Jersey

Children
(Based on 'The Storm' by Walter de la Mare)

First there were 16 of us, then there were 20 of us,
Then there were many more.
All of us happy, cheerful children,
Heading out through the huge door.
And the sea got rough and the breeze got higher.
As it came up with a powerful squeak.
With 10 of us - 20 of us,
Children listening to the seashore.

Mitchell Thebault (8)
St John's School, Jersey

I Like . . .

I like the taste of sweet popcorn crunching on my teeth
I like the smell of dark chocolate rushing up my nose
I like the feel of white cushions tickling my face
I like the sound of brown leaves crunching in my ears
I like the sight of computers flashing at my eyes.

Ella Averty (7)
St John's School, Jersey

I Like . . .

I like the taste of candyfloss tickling my chin
I like the smell of chewy orange mash in my mouth
I like the feel of a zebra, soft and smooth on my hand
I like the sight of rabbits hopping around my garden.

Jocey Dibbens (8)
St John's School, Jersey

The Sunny Day
(Based on 'The Storm' by Walter de la Mare)

First there were three of us, then there were five of us,
Then there were many more.
All of us boiling and cheerful animals,
Heading out through the minute door.
And the sea rose and the wind blew,
As it came up with a terrific roar.
With three of us - five of us - eight of us,
Animals listening to the seashore.

Henri Helie-Merrony (8)
St John's School, Jersey

I Like . . .

I like the taste of sweet popcorn crunching on my teeth
I like the smell of sweet candy flickering up my nose
I like the feel of water splashing on my face
I like the sound of a violin playing soft music in my ears
I like the sight of Christmas lights flickering in my eyes.

Abbie Roberts (7)
St John's School, Jersey

I Like . . .

I like the taste of brown chocolate crunching in my mouth
I like the smell of warm pasta drizzling up my nose
I like the feel of soft fur rolling down my cheek
I like the sound of noisy laughter filling up my ears
I like the sight of disco lights twinkling in my eyes.

Ruby Mason (7)
St John's School, Jersey

Dogs
(Based on 'The Storm' by Walter de la Mare)

First there were eight of us, then there were ten of us,
Then there were eleven dogs more.
All of them panting, frightened dogs,
Heading through the outrageous door.
And the dogs barked as the door rang,
As it came up with an ear-breaking roar.
With eight of us, ten of us, eleven of us,
Running along the seashore.

Megan McCabe (8)
St John's School, Jersey

I Like . . .

I like the taste of buttery popcorn crackling on my tongue
I like the sound of my fat dog barking in my ears
I like the smell of sweet candyfloss
I like the feel of the hot sun while I sunbathe on the sand
I like the sight of the streetlights flashing at night.

Daniel Hillion (7)
St John's School, Jersey

I Like . . .

I like the taste of sticky toffee sticking on my tongue
I like the smell of hot chips nuzzling at my nose
I like the feel of cold blood trickling down my leg
I like the sound of loud music rocking in my ears
I like the sight of cool TV programmes sparkling in my eyes.

Benjamin Fosse (7)
St John's School, Jersey

Adults On The Run
(Based on 'The Storm' by Walter de la Mare)

First there were 9 of us, then there were 20 of us,
Then there were a dozen adults more.
All of us happy, joyful,
Heading out the tiny door.
And the sea splashed and the wind rose.
As it came up with a loud crash,
With 9 of us - 20 of us - eight of us,
Adults listening to the sea roar.

Owen Harper (8)
St John's School, Jersey

I Like . . .

I like the taste of chewy, sour sweets fizzing on my tongue
I like the smell of petrol tingling up my nose
I like the feel of my gran's fluffy cat rubbing on my hand
I like the sound of my dog's collar jingling in my ears
I like the sight of the lovely red sunset in the morning.

Maxwell Friend (8)
St John's School, Jersey

I Like . . .

I like the taste of sausages sizzling on my tongue
I like the smell of candyfloss whizzing in the machine
I like the feel of water dripping down my hands
I like the sound of robin redbreasts singing in my ear
I like the sight of white owls twittering in the trees.

Todd Stanier (8)
St John's School, Jersey

Seascape

S alty sea washes away the algae and the foam hovers over the
sea edge
E ven the smoothness of the bladder-wrack rises quietly
to the surface
A s the children throw pebbles into the sea, they skim across the
shimmering water
S creaming gulls diving and swooping around people, nearly eating
their ice cream
C hildren are smiling and having fun while building their sandcastles,
and as they fall down, they crumble like a broken cracker
A bove all the people on the beach, some people have a bird's-eye
view and say, 'We're going there tomorrow,'
P op! goes someone's ice cream which they are going to enjoy -
a delightful, tasty ice cream
E veryone is heading home. They have had a really good time
building their sandcastles and eating their ice creams, but now it's
time to say goodbye to the people and say hello to the dogs.

Hannah Couriard (10)
St John's School, Jersey

I Like . . .

I like the taste of yummy white chocolate melting in my throat
I like the smell of lovely brown ice cream sailing up my nose
I like the feel of my lovely soft teddy brushing my hands
I like the sound of the quiet sea washing against my feet
I like the sight of St Brelades beach at night, glittering against
                                                                             my eyes.

Jodie Barry (7)
St John's School, Jersey

If I Were A Human Transformer

I would transform into a puppy.
I would glide frantically.
I would sprint fiercely.
I would swoop dramatically.
I would fly amazingly.
I would roar viciously.
People would adore me and love me in every way.
Everyone would cheer for me.
If only I were a human transformer.

Olivia Bouchard (8)
St John's School, Jersey

If I Were An Elf . . .

I would tiptoe invisibly and silently around rooms
I would sneak colourful sweets out of the cupboard
I would call people around to my house and have secret parties
I would breathe heavily
I would play carefully with my friends
I would swim quickly for miles.

If only I were an elf!

Teigan Purkiss (8)
St John's School, Jersey

If I Were A Devil . . .

I would be reckless and I would destructively destroy people
I would quickly sprint as fast as a cheetah
If anyone saw me they would scream loudly and run away quickly
I would be as quiet as a mouse
I would stamp as hard as a giant and move slowly

If I were a devil.

Max Haslam (8)
St John's School, Jersey

Colour Poem

Red is bright and it makes me think of roses
Orange is light but it makes me want to fight
Yellow is funny and it makes me feel so sunny
Green is mean like an evil queen
Blue is cool so let's have a dip in the pool
Purple is fun so let's have a plum
Black is a snake for my aching back
White is a fright in the middle of the night.

Caitlin Harris (9)
St Luke's Primary School, Jersey

Colour Poem

Red is bright, rosy and vibrant
Orange is light, bright and the sunset
Yellow is light, sunny and juicy
Green is grass, leafy and colourful
Blue is shiny, the sky and colourful
Purple is girlie, can be dark and nice
Black is dark, miserable and boyish
White is light, hard to see and peaceful.

Jade McCormack (9)
St Luke's Primary School, Jersey

Colour Poem

Red is bright and shiny
Orange is fizzy and bubbly
Yellow is sunny and hot
Green is soft and pointy
Blue is clear and wet
Purple is velvety and sparkly
Black is dark and crowded
White is peaceful and quiet.

Chloë Portch (9)
St Luke's Primary School, Jersey

Dirty Water

Dirty Water is a muddy, mucky and diseased person.
He makes me feel sick and unclean.
His face looks muddy, dry, dirty and disgusting.
His eyes look tired and covered in mud.
His mouth is mucky, he has black teeth and muddy lips.
His hair is brown and damp.
His clothes are made out of muddy, dry, charity clothes.
When he moves, he drags his feet along.
When he speaks, bugs and mud come out of his mouth.
He lives in a muddy cave on his own.
Dirty Water makes me feel sick.

Sands-Alicia Sangan (10)
St Luke's Primary School, Jersey

Cheerful

Cheerful is a lovely lady.
She makes me feel happy and safe inside.
Her face looks like there's a big change in her.
Her eyes are like green rubies.
Her mouth is a big, red cherry.
Her hair is gold like the sun.
Her clothes are made of pink and green stars.
When she moves you can hear her high heels.
When she speaks it's like I'm in a different world.
She lives in a palace with her mum and pet cat.
Cheerful makes me feel over the moon.

Mary Melaugh (10)
St Luke's Primary School, Jersey

Clean Water

Clean Water is a happy, jumpy person, like a best friend
She makes me feel lucky
Her face looks clean and innocent like a little girl
Her eyes are blue and sparkly like a summer's day
Her mouth is pink like icing
Her hair is long and curly
She wears turquoise, silk dresses
When she moves she glides like a beautiful dolphin
When she speaks she sings a song of happiness
Clean Water is loved by everyone.

Katie Longman (10)
St Luke's Primary School, Jersey

Floods

Is a giant creature
He makes me feel scared
His face looks big, round and evil
His eyes are as blue as sapphires
His mouth has round, curly lips
His hair is long and curvy
His clothes are made of thick water
When he moves he rushes like a current
When he speaks he shouts out loud
He lives in a mansion with his wet friends and his old furniture
He makes me scared.

Bradley Welsh-Falle (10)
St Luke's Primary School, Jersey

Dirty Water

Dirty Water is a mean and nasty person
He makes me feel scared and sick
His face looks thin, pointy and is as brown as chocolate
His eyes are furious red
His mouth is like a frown of barbecue sauce
His hair is brown with bugs and knots
His clothes are made of crunchy mud which falls off and crumbles
When he moves it's like a slug spreading illness
When he speaks it's low and he spits out horror
He lives in a big, brown river alone
I hate Dirty Water.

Megan Buxton (10)
St Luke's Primary School, Jersey

Winter

Winter is a bad person
He makes me feel sad and cold
He is bad because he steals the heat
His face looks frozen and bad
His eyes are an icy colour
His mouth is blue with icicles as fangs
His hair is frozen solid
He moves very slowly and makes a loud noise
When he speaks he turns things to ice
He lives in an ice cave
I hate Winter.

Taylor Cairns (10)
St Luke's Primary School, Jersey

Clean Water

Clean Water is a beautiful creature
She makes me feel happy and joyful
Her face looks soft and silky
Her eyes are as blue as crystals
Her mouth is sparkly and clean
Her hair reminds me of shiny glass
Her clothes are made of silk and
When she moves, she leaves everything sparkling
When she speaks, it sounds very sweet
She lives in a big castle with shiny windows and glittery curtains
Clean Water is nice to me.

Paige-Aisha Du Feu (10)
St Luke's Primary School, Jersey

Happiness

Happiness is a kind little girl
She makes me feel warm and happy
Her face looks kind and comforting
Her eyes are as blue as sapphires
Her lips are as red as roses
Her hair is as white as snow
Her clothes are made of pink flower petals
When she moves, she bounces along
When she speaks, she sounds like an angel
She lives in a pink castle with her mum and dad
Happiness likes me.

Caitlin Day (10)
St Luke's Primary School, Jersey

Flood

Flood is a mean murderer
He makes me feel sad and scared
His face looks like a giant wave
His eyes are leftovers from the beach or the river
His mouth is a lost surfboard
His hair is bald as a wave
His clothes are made of the whirlpools
When he speaks, it's like the silent wind
When he moves, it's a tide that is pushed in
He lives in an underwater cave with sea animals
And he feels mad to be trapped there.

Connor Pinel (10)
St Luke's Primary School, Jersey

Clean Water

Clean Water is a relief of thirst
She makes me feel safe and clean
Her face looks shiny and clear
Her eyes are blue and clean
Her mouth is wet, not dry, not thirst, just calm
Her hair is crystal-blue like the ocean on a hot day
Her clothes are made of velvet blowing in the wind
When she moves, she runs like a tidal wave
When she speaks, she gargles with clean water
She lives in a ship with flags and parties
Water cleans me.

Katie Veitch (10)
St Luke's Primary School, Jersey

Clean Water

Clean Water is a kind person.
She makes me feel happy and safe.
Her face looks really pretty.
Her eyes are sky-blue.
Her mouth is clean and shiny.
Her hair is brown and straight.
Her clothes are made of silk.
When she moves, she tiptoes around.
When she speaks, she is very quiet.
She lives in a crystal, clean and clear.
She is kind to me.

Keera De Sousa (10)
St Luke's Primary School, Jersey

Night

Night is a dark man
He makes me feel scared
His face looks like an ogre
His eyes are as red as rubies
His mouth is really big with four fangs
His hair is as dark as night
His clothes are made of leather
When he moves, he does not make a sound
When he speaks it is really quiet
He lives in a cave with bats and a wolf
Night scares me.

Alex Stout (11)
St Luke's Primary School, Jersey

Night

Night is a kind, gentle, caring person.
She makes me feel warm, calm and safe.
Her face looks like a round, happy face that's always smiling.
Her eyes are beautiful, blue crystals glowing in the sun.
Her mouth is like a bold cherry, always wet.
Her hair is like golden curls sitting on her shoulder.
Her clothes are made of silver and gold.
When she moves, she bounces gracefully like a balloon.
When she speaks, she uses a soft voice, so gentle and calm.
She lives in a palace with Mum and Dad.
Night makes me feel happy.

Ella Glasgow (10)
St Luke's Primary School, Jersey

Dreams

Dreams is a lovely lady.
She makes me feel safe and happy.
Her face looks like an angel.
Her eyes are blue diamonds.
Her lips and hair are both shiny and soft.
Her clothes are made of silk.
She gracefully flies over the town.
When she speaks, a lovely voice rises.
She lives in a beautiful place with flowers everywhere.

Janine McBain (10)
St Luke's Primary School, Jersey

Cake

There once was a young frog called Puddles
Who had a best friend called Muddles
She made a mistake
And ate Puddle's cake
And then didn't get very nice cuddles.

Jessica Nelson (10)
St Luke's Primary School, Jersey

Alex

Alex is a crazy guitarist raging to play.
Alex is Hawaii always welcoming me.
She is a sofa giving me warm hugs.
Her hair is a soft, polar bear's fur.
She smells of a daring daisy.
Her voice is an angel singing hip-hop on a groovy guitar.
Alex wears butterfly's wings and silk.
Alex is midday, the time of day when she's just warming up.
Alex is spaghetti, always all over the place
And is apple pie and vanilla ice cream.
She's sweetness, full of it, from painted toenails to golden hair.

Martha Noble (9)
St Swithun's RC Primary School, Southsea

Hippopotamus

A hippopotamus is a naughty child rolling in the mud.
A hippopotamus is a warrior charging at his enemies.
A hippopotamus is my mother in law as loud as a baby's scream.
A hippopotamus is an old lady just forgotten to wash.
A hippopotamus is a young child splashing in the bath.
A hippopotamus is a young man-charmer going on a date.

Jude Keating (9)
St Swithun's RC Primary School, Southsea

My Colours

As white as a dove flying high in the blue sky.
As green as a tall, waving tree in the wind.
As blue as seawater on a boiling hot day.
As pink as the Pink Panther running around on TV.

Jack Yeats (10)
St Swithun's RC Primary School, Southsea

Ten Things Found In A Witch's Pocket

A sparkling night complete with six silky stars and one full moon.
A travelling machine that takes you into your dreams.
A fluffy cloud of feathers to snuggle in to when you are cold.
A deafening banshee to scare away good children
on a summer's night.
The word 'diflehie' - no one knows what it means.
A bag of darkness to smother the night in.
A book of bad spells to make the world a terrible place.
A bag of planets like Jupiter and Mars.
A magic finger that ruins your life.
A moth to keep you company when you are lonely.

Ellie Dommersen (10)
St Swithun's RC Primary School, Southsea

Six Things Found In A Footballer's Bag

A Premiership ball from the game.
A pair of golden boots that scored the winning goal.
A Pompey kit covered in mud after the game.
Sweaty shin pads sticking to your legs.
Some keeper's gloves tipping the ball over the bar for a corner.
A water bottle ready for the game.

Oscar Chase (10)
St Swithun's RC Primary School, Southsea

Goblin Treasure

A sharp pencil covered in blood
A knife with graffiti on the blade
A bottle of deadly poisoned water
Dolls - Voodoo dolls with poor people
A phone to threaten the innocent.

Wiktor Karolewski (10)
St Swithun's RC Primary School, Southsea

Six Things Found In Mr Mackay's Rucksack

In Mr Mackay's rucksack . . .
He cares for his family photo,
Which is smothered in love and happy memories.
A golden key, unlocking a secret, magical world,
Which only he can visit.
A small teddy bear from his childhood,
Bought for him by his mother and father,
To represent their love for him.
A pair of sparkling diamond earrings worn by his wife
On their wedding day.
His most special and colourful tie
Worn by him at his eldest son's graduation.
His 24 carat gold ring that he will treasure forever
And pass down to his future descendants.

Freya Hardcastle & Ella Blay (9)
St Swithun's RC Primary School, Southsea

What Is Blue?

What is blue?
The Irish Sea is blue
Deep down jellyfish live

What is white?
A heron is white
Pecking in the sand for rag and lug worms

What is red?
A devil's stick is red
Cursing every good soul

What is gold?
A goblin's chamber has gold in it
Without the real world knowing

What is black?
A cat with bright yellow eyes
Prowling in the starry night.

Michael Olive (10)
St Swithun's RC Primary School, Southsea

Nine Things In My Mum's Handbag

A lipstick as red as a rose.
A pack of chewing gum waiting to be opened.
A blue pen wriggling all around.
A mobile phone vibrating and shaking the whole bag.
A newly bought pair of earrings sparkling in the lonely darkness of the bag.
A shiny, purple sweet watching nothing, waiting to be eaten.
A purse jingling and jangling because of the money inside.
A banana hoping to be snaffled by a monkey.
A mascara as black as a dark night.

Olivia Campion (9)
St Swithun's RC Primary School, Southsea

Our Head Teacher

Our head teacher is precious treasure under the sea
She's a chuckling schoolgirl always having a laugh
She's an angel in the blue sky

Miss Jones is a sunflower letting her love shine
She's a purring kitten on my lap

Miss Jones is a shiny star
Shooting from the sky.

Jessica Cooper (9)
St Swithun's RC Primary School, Southsea

Six Things In An Elf's Handbag

A present wrapped up in shiny, silver silk
A tooth as white as snow
A hat all pink and small
A page of children that are good
And a page of children that have been bad
A picture of Santa and the whole family.

Ella Mallinder (9)
St Swithun's RC Primary School, Southsea

The Writer Of This Poem
(Based on 'The Writer of this Poem' by Roger McGough)

The writer of this poem
Is taller than a baby giraffe
As ready as the broom awaiting its witch
As gorgeous as a rock star!

As bold as a rose in a daisy patch
As sharp as the tip of a knife
As strong as a crocodile
As tricky as a stitch.

As smooth as a pebble
As quick as a flash
As clean as Marmite (the rabbit)
As clever as Marcia.

The writer of this poem
Is very nice
But she bids you good day
So leave in a trice!

Lauren Nicholls (10)
St Swithun's RC Primary School, Southsea

Hallowe'en Poem

Watch out for the vampires,
Watch out for the bats,
Watch out for the ghosts and ghouls
And the mighty *rat!*
Beware the hooded strangers,
Beware the scarlet gnats,
But most of all . . .
Beware the vicious *vampire cat!*
Avoid the dark, creepy woods,
Avoid the brimstone bog,
Avoid the scary alleyways,
But most of all . . .
Avoid the *talking log!*

Isobel Johnson (10)
St Swithun's RC Primary School, Southsea

What Are Our Favourite Colours?

What on Earth is blue?
The flowing waters of the River Thames
As it weaves its way through the city of London.

What is green?
The leaf of an oak tree as it falls swirling to the ground.

What the hell is red?
The Red Devils of Manchester United
As they run out onto the freshly cut pitch for the Cup Final.

What is brown?
Sausages sizzling in the frying pan for my breakfast.
The smell makes my mouth water and my tummy rumble.

What is pink?
The colour of my uncooked bacon that I'll be eating with my sausages.

What is purple?
Blackcurrant squash.
It's not my favourite but it tastes quite nice.

What is orange?
My goldfish Fred
Who swims through tunnels and caves in his tank.

What is black?
The smooth coat of Basil, Mr Parker's cute Labrador dog,
As shiny as a glossy photograph.

Joshua Humphries & Michael Cox-Smith (11)
St Swithun's RC Primary School, Southsea

What Is Pink?

What is pink?
A baby bunny's ears listening to new sounds of the world.

What is orange?
An orange is orange just being freshly peeled.

What is red?
A fresh strawberry is red, when it is being carried back from Devon.

What is blue?
The sea is blue, glistening in the blazing sun.

What is green?
The succulent, tender grapes are green, freshly picked by a
                                                    gentle girl.

What is yellow?
A ripened banana is yellow, sitting in the silver, shining fruit bowl.

What is white?
The French football team's T-shirts are white, just before the
                                                    game begins.

What is brown?
Chocolate is brown, drizzling from the fountain in Thornton's
                                                    chocolate shop.

What is violet?
Petals are violet, being thrown across the wedding isle,
(To celebrate the new life together they have ahead of them).

Elysia Gill (11) & Darcy Leake (10)
St Swithun's RC Primary School, Southsea

What Is Orange?

What is orange?
A carrot is orange
Being cut up by a worn-out mother.

What is purple?
An angry person's face is purple
As she shouts at her crying child like an angry bull.

What is blue?
A beautifully calm sea is blue
As it gently washes against the craggy cliffs.

What is black?
A ravenously raving storm is black
As it looks down hungrily on the poor world.

What is grey?
Gatwick airport floor is grey
As people with dirty shoes stride manfully across the just
                                                          polished floor.

What is pink?
Reese Witherspoon's gorgeous outfit in Legally Blonde
And Legally Blonde 2 is pink.

What is yellow?
A deliciously bitter lemon is yellow
Freshly squeezed on wonderful pancakes.

What is green?
The cool grass is green
As the cold rain softly patters down.

Grace Goble (10)
St Swithun's RC Primary School, Southsea

My Magic Box
(Based on 'Magic Box' by Kit Wright)

I will put in my box . . .

A never-ending summer filled with golden light,
A baby's first word spoken from her bright pink lips,
The sight of a clear, blue waterfall rushing down golden rocks.

I will put in my box . . .

A pitch-black night glistening with silver stars all through the night,
My granny that I never got to meet,
The gallop of a silver unicorn rushing through stars.

I will put in my box . . .

The sound of a baby dolphin having the best time ever,
A pearl that glistens at the bottom of a deep blue sea
And a mermaid's scale that shines like a thousand stars
And it never stops shining.

My box is fashioned from . . .

Rubies, gold and pearls,
With sapphires on the lid
And magic dust in the corners.
Its hinges are made from the pearly-white teeth of sharks.

I shall surf on my box
Over an Australian blue sea
And wash up onto a Caribbean island
Covered with palm trees,
With coconuts and the juiciest mangos there could ever be.

Hermione Green (10)
St Swithun's RC Primary School, Southsea

What Is Blue?

What is blue?
A Pompey home shirt is blue,
Even when covered in mud.

What is red?
A freshly cut scar is red,
All dripping with blood.

What is green?
Trampled grass is green
In the local park.

What is white?
A newborn baby Dalmatian is white,
Letting out its very first bark.

What is yellow?
Ripe bananas are yellow,
Eaten up by a cheeky chimpanzee.

What is orange?
Marmalade is orange,
Put on toast for someone's tea.

What is violet?
Clouds are violet,
Floating towards the sparkling sea.

What is pink?
Skin is pink,
On the cap of your knee.

Guy Elder (10)
St Swithun's RC Primary School, Southsea

What Is White?

What is white?
A fluffy cloud is white,
Floating constantly in the illuminating, blue sky.

What is green?
Leaves are green,
Waving and spinning in the breeze
On their lovely tree.

What is yellow?
The sun is yellow,
Burning furiously all the time
In space and sky.

What is red?
The sunset is red,
Burning the hours of darkness
With rays of light.

What is blue?
The sea is blue,
Sinking and smashing many boats.
(The sea is engulfing its dinner!)

What is pink?
He is pink,
His face brewing red
As he reacts to his irritation.

What is orange?
Americans are orange,
Tanned so much
They begin to go pale.

Samuel Madden (9)
St Swithun's RC Primary School, Southsea

What Is White?

What is white?
A dove is white,
Drifting elegantly through the darkness of night.

What is yellow?
The sparkling sun shining bright on the glorious world below.

What is brown?
Some crispy leaves falling slowly but gently onto the fresh,
                                                                             green grass.

What is blue?
Why, beautiful dolphins are blue, with a small sparkle in their
                                                                             dark eyes.

What is red?
A sunset is red, shining brightly overhead in the view.

What is pink?
A baby's special toy is pink before being ripped and scuffed up
                                                       by the cheeky, black puppy.

Alice Chatband (11)
St Swithun's RC Primary School, Southsea

What Is Blue?

What is blue?
Blue is a storm in November
On an immense, gloomy, unfathomable day.

What is green?
A haze of green, succulent grass
With gigantic green flowers waiting to be eaten.

What is orange?
The sky is orange waiting for the sun
To go to the other side.

Thomas Rix (9)
St Swithun's RC Primary School, Southsea

What Is Blue?

What is blue?
A Pompey shirt is blue worn by a true fan of football
Swaying, in the southern air stream.

What is green?
An Irish shamrock is green, chosen for the Irish symbol.

What is red?
Flames are red, lighting up our only hope.

What is black?
Space is black, rolling around the universe like a black tyre.

What is white?
Shaun the Sheep is white, small and puffy, but clever and funny.

What is yellow?
The sun is yellow, forever shining over us,
Finally it turns into a red dwarf.

Peter Jacobs (9)
St Swithun's RC Primary School, Southsea

Yellow Is . . .

What is yellow?
Yellow is a freshly picked daisy growing in the field.

What is red?
Red is a strawberry from Devon travelling to Portsmouth.

What is pink?
Pink is a baby bird cracking open its shell.

What is purple?
Purple is a juicy grape in the fruit bowl.

What is green?
Green is a leaf falling from a tree.

What is blue?
The sea is blue, reflecting the sun.

Emilie Duda (10)
St Swithun's RC Primary School, Southsea

What Is Pink?

What is pink?
The Pink Panther is pink,
Strutting across the television in his own style of strangeness.

What is blue?
The deep blue sea is blue,
Crashing against dark Blue Mountain with snow covering the peak
of it.

What is green?
Sweet-smelling grass is green,
Swishing in green glory in the dark soil.

What is red?
Fresh-smelling plants are red,
Waving in the light, lovely wind.

What is yellow?
The sun is yellow,
Brightly shining in the desert where the sand lies softly.

What is black?
The dark, gloomy night,
Where wolves rampage,
Savagely ripping apart every animal in their path.

Louis Lawson (9)
St Swithun's RC Primary School, Southsea

The Beast

A beast with eyes as large as jewels
Fur that feels like silk
And in the moonlight turns silver
Teeth like stars captured in its mouth
It slips away
Disappearing in the moonlight like magic.

Alex Fowler (10)
St Swithun's RC Primary School, Southsea

The Writer Of This Poem
(Based on 'The Writer of this Poem' by Roger McGough)

The writer of this poem is . . .
Taller than a mountain reaching its frost-covered arms up to the sky.
As keen as a bird ready to learn to fly up into the breezy air.
As vain as a lion gazing in the mirror and brushing its long,
                                                        wavy mane.

As bold as a single fish lying in the lonely depths of the ocean.
As sharp as the words of a bully being spoken nastily and coldly.
As strong as the universe struggling to spin all the planets on
                                          each finger like basketballs.
As tricky as a hard sum being solved cautiously and carefully.
As smooth as the surface of a freshly cleaned floor with the sunrays
                                  reflecting on it, glittering and shining.
As quick as a hare, darting across a flower-covered field.
As clean as a T-shirt, brand new and blinding people everywhere
                                                                it goes.
As clever as a scientist who has just discovered how to
                                          solve pollution.

'The writer of this poem
Never ceases to amaze
She's one in a million billion
(Or so the poem says!)'

Chloe Hinton (10)
St Swithun's RC Primary School, Southsea

Our Head Teacher

Mrs Jones is a golden rainbow.
She is a pearl in the deep blue sea.
She is the moon shining in the dark blue sky.
She is a chrysanthemum swaying in the breeze.
She is a soft kitten mewing.
She is the delicate scent of a rose.
She is a little hedgehog rolled into a ball.

Angela Gorman (9)
St Swithun's RC Primary School, Southsea

The Writer Of This Poem

(Based on 'The Writer of this Poem' by Roger McGough)

The writer of this poem
Is as tall as a baby giraffe
As keen as a superstar
As beautiful as a china doll

As bold as a lioness
As sharp as a knife
As tough as old boots
As tricky as a fib

As smooth as marble
As quick as a snake
As cheeky as a monkey
As thin as a rake

'The writer of this poem
Never ceases to amaze
She is one out of a million
Or so the poem says.'

Hannah Haughey (10)
St Swithun's RC Primary School, Southsea

What Is Blue?

What is blue?
Blue is a sea spinning around like a storm.

What is blue?
Blue is the sky shining so bright.

What is blue?
Blue is flying like a bright bird.

What is blue?
Blue is the ocean,
Crashing waves so high that anyone would drown.

Francy Augustine (9)
St Swithun's RC Primary School, Southsea

The Writer Of This Poem
(Based on 'The Writer of this Poem' by Roger McGough)

The writer of this poem
Is taller than a post
As keen as ketchup
As handsome as a ghost

As bold as a tree
As sharp as pain
As strong as can be
As tricky as a game

As smooth as a curl
As quick as a bat
As clean as a pearl
As clever as a cat

'The writer of this poem
Never ceases to amaze
He's one in a billion
(Or so the poem says!)'

Jack Hardcastle (11)
St Swithun's RC Primary School, Southsea

My Sister

My sister is as hot as fire
And is crazy about her toy hippo
She is nearly as fast as me
And as cuddly as a feather down pillow

She wears the same outfit for more than a week
Her eyes are coloured like melted chocolate
Every time I listen to music, she dances and leaps
And is as crazy as a clown

My sister cares for me when I'm ill
She cheers me up when I'm sad
My sister won't tell me off if I'm bad
My sister is the best.

Molly McMaster (9)
St Swithun's RC Primary School, Southsea

My Magic Box
(Based on 'Magic Box' by Kit Wright)

A leather blanket the size of an elephant
The ripple of bright blue water on a summer's day
And all the dangers in the world

The yellow eye of a dragon
And a book of time travel
And the Devil as a hairy biker

My box is fashioned from platinum, ice and gold
With a platinum handle on the lid
And everlasting chocolate in the corners
Its hinges are made of diamonds
With pearls in the middle.

I will hang glide upside down on my box
Across the Atlantic on my box to Jamaica
On the other side
And live in paradise forever.

Christopher Shore (9)
St Swithun's RC Primary School, Southsea

Adam

He's a playful puppy accidentally breaking things.
He's a T-rex shaking the world with a roar.
He's a bouncy bean.
He's a still statue sometimes.
He's an artist with a crayon.
He's a little runner.
He's a pepperoni pizza, scrummy to taste.
He's a spoonful of jelly.
He's a soft, little teddy, my Adam is!

Josephine Lake (9)
St Swithun's RC Primary School, Southsea

My Magic Box
(Based on 'Magic Box' by Kit Wright)

I will put in my box . . .

The first heartbeat of a tin man
The last breath of a giant grey elephant
The everlasting, fearless sky watching every birth and death

I will put in my box . . .

The sound of a cold, lonely mountain grumbling
A great oak tree reaching to take a juicy apple
A piece of rock floating in the utter darkness of space

I will put in my box . . .

A German bomb scarring the sky and exploding
As a firework of death
A dehydrated traveller stumbling towards a fresh oasis
The beautiful, blue blossom fluttering in spring

I will put in my box . . .

A lion's fierce roar stunning the jungle
A ruby-red scarf softly brushing pale skin
A cup of clear, crystal water from the rushing river

My box is fashioned from . . .

Stars and jewels and Egyptian cloth
With Roman coins in the corners
Its hinges are styled with wood and ancient writing

I shall surf on my box
Through lands and countries
Summers and winters
Then I shall lie on the ice
With my box slightly opening
Letting out past, present and future.

Emma Ford (10)
St Swithun's RC Primary School, Southsea

The Writer Of This Poem
(Based on 'The Writer of this Poem' by Roger McGough)

The writer of this poem
Is taller than an old oak tree
As keen as a famous footballer
As handsome as can be

As bold as a punching bag
As sharp as an angry shark's teeth
As strong as a huge wrestler
As tricky as a riddle

As smooth as soft felt
As quick as a squirrel
As clean as mountain water
As clever as a computer

'The writer of this poem
Never ceases to amaze
He's one in a million billion
(Or so the poem says).'

Anita Ghosh (9)
St Swithun's RC Primary School, Southsea

The Magic Box
(Based on 'Magic Box' by Kit Wright)

I will put in my box . . .

A shining light from under my pillow
A scale from a Norwegian sweep back
A toe born from a fire-breathing dragon.

I will put in my box . . .

My grandad who went up a million miles away
A dying man in a misted desert
A person who came out of the dead.

How I will travel with the box . . .

I will surf through the air dodging the birds as I go
We will go to the Caribbean and go wind surfing
And go on the aeroplane back home.

My box is made from golden silk,
Silver and dragon scales.

Harry Burn (9)
St Swithun's RC Primary School, Southsea

My Magic Box
(Based on 'Magic Box' by Kit Wright)

In my magic box I will possess . . .

A raindrop from the first fall of night
A twinkling eye from the first Queen of England
And the first tree of creation.

I will hold in my magic box . . .

The sun that shines so golden
The white, whirling wedding dress my mother wore
And the sound of singing bluebells.

In my magic box I will look after . . .

A sizzling sweet which I will eat in 100 years
The golden hair that was my mother's
And melted chocolate that is the last of its kind.

Inside my magic box I will defend . . .

The darkness and sorrow of a dead soldier's body
The heart of an innocent man
And a cobweb from a dark cellar.

My box is fashioned from . . .

Cocoa bark that still smells
And silky spiders' webs that never break
With bluebell flowers on the lid
And silver wrapping paper.
The hinges are dust and sand
My first feeling
The secret traps make sure my pure, white moon is safe
Ruby-red crystals cover the side.

I shall travel with my box to . . .

The pyramids of Egypt which happen to be haunted
The wonderful, wavy, blue sea
And the new game ball basket.

My box is my best friend!

Azzurra Moores (9)
St Swithun's RC Primary School, Southsea

The Magic Box
(Based on 'Magic Box' by Kit Wright)

I will put in the box . . .

The first fresh laugh of a baby
The first steps of a baby giraffe
The last joke of a joker
A little piece of the bright golden sun that shines upon everything

I will put in the box . . .

The beautiful, shiny moon that saw and sees every birth and death
The first song ever sung by a mermaid
The first bark of a puppy
The last boiling breath of the last dragon ever

I will put in the box . . .

The first tooth ever picked up by the tooth fairy
The colourful hat of an elf
A stunning, white Greek unicorn
A witch's broomstick

I will put in the box . . .

Santa Claus' thick, big, black belt
The first and last footstep of the first giant
A shiny, bright yellow star from the sky

My box is fashioned from silk, white and gold
Steel birds on the lid
And full of secrets in Latin in the corners.
Its hinges are made out of iron
From the ruins of the Iron Man.

I shall surf on my box
Through time and space
And to wonderful place.

Carolina Gonzalez (10)
St Swithun's RC Primary School, Southsea

The Magic Box
(Based on 'Magic Box' by Kit Wright)

I will magic these into my magic box
A rabbit with a fluffy tail
A shooting star flying like Peter Pan
A pot of leprechaun's gold at the end of a rainbow
Milk chocolate spreading everywhere
And the world made of chocolate.

I will gently put into my magic box
A *big*, tall snowman,
White and cold like a freezer
Freezing like an ice cream
And a man's heart in the snowman
With a little tiny hat.

Our magic box is made from
Magic stars of quilt and cotton buds
And lovely pictures of fish
With perfumed hearts on the lid
Wishing wishes in the corners.
Its hinges are leather.

I shall discover the world on my magic box
To Canada to Wales
And to everywhere else.

Ellie Langton (9) & Gillian
St Swithun's RC Primary School, Southsea

The Magic Box
(Based on 'Magic Box' by Kit Wright)

I will put in my box . . .

A strand of the mane of the most golden lion,
A leaf from a tree in the Amazon,
A sip of the water from the River Nile,
The silky fur of my hamster.

I will put in my box . . .

A handful of the coldest snow from the French Alps,
The fragrance of my mum's perfume,
A dog on a pony,
A baboon on a bike.

I will put in my box . . .

A fresh loaf of bread baked by the finest bakers,
The first smile of a newborn baby,
The heat from a dragon's nostrils,
A squid on a stick,
The sweet smell of a rambling rose,
The gold from the end of a rainbow.

My box is fashioned from the finest oak bark
With flies and snails in the corners.
Its hinges are tissue paper.

I shall surf on my box
Over the Pacific Ocean to Krakatoa
And live the rest of my life on the beach.

Joshua Cooper (10)
St Swithun's RC Primary School, Southsea

The Magic Box
(Based on 'Magic Box' by Kit Wright)

I will put in my box . . .

The beautiful smile of my mum's shining face
When I make her laugh.
The taste of sweet milk chocolate
That melts down my eyelid.
The scale of a fabulous mermaid swimming by the sea.

I will put in my box . . .

The first teardrop of a newborn baby in hospital.
The blazing sun shining on everyone.
A piece of ice melting away a summer's night.

My box is fashioned from . . .

Love hearts, flowers and stars,
With a big diamond on the lid
And a rose on the corners.

Its hinges are the sound of a newborn baby girl on the Earth.

I shall surf in my box over the hot great pyramid of Giza.

Naima Reza (10)
St Swithun's RC Primary School, Southsea

My Magic Box
(Based on 'Magic Box' by Kit Wright)

In my magic box I will keep . . .

The sabretooth eyes of a dragon
The swift movement of a panther running
The balance of a bird searching for worms
The mist on the top of a mountain
The darkest layers of a cave
The flame from the burning sun
The wetness of the sea spraying over the rocks
The roar of a flying creature
The shell of an ancient tortoise
And a piece of an alien ship.

My box is fashioned from . . .

Fire and water and earth
With dust on the lid and sunlight in the corners
Its hinges are made from a pterodactyl's wings.

I shall surf on my box through the wide, thrashing sea
And onto a shining, yellow beach
Where coconuts are dangling limply from the branches.

George Gooding (9)
St Swithun's RC Primary School, Southsea

The Magic Box
(Based on 'Magic Box' by Kit Wright)

In my magic box I will keep . . .

All my friends' giggles when they're happy,
The first silver snowflake on a gentle winter's eve,
The shiniest golden star of an autumn night,
The hug from all my family when they are as happy as can be.

I will put in my box . . .

The fur of my black and white cats,
The dust of a silent fairy flying through the air,
The luck of a little, green leprechaun,
The wish of an *ancient* Japanese dragon
And the hop of a cheeky little pixie.

I'll put in my box . . .

The first wink of a baby boy when he came out of his
                                   mother's tummy,
The rumbling belly of a golden dog,
A horn of a sparkling unicorn.

My box is fashioned from ice, silver and copper,
With stars on the lid and wishes in the corner.
Its hinges are made from the oldest tin in Japan.

I shall surf on my box over the sun and the moon
And land on a star
Watching the whole world with my box beside me.

Kiera Quickfall (10)
St Swithun's RC Primary School, Southsea

The Magic Box
(Based on 'Magic Box' by Kit Wright)

I will put in my box . . .

The tears of a baby as it awaits its mother
The paws of a lion that walks the savannah
The wings of an eagle that explores its surroundings

I will put in my box . . .

The sweet sounds of the robin on a blossom tree
The hunger of poor people begging for food
The sound of children when they laugh gloriously

I will put in my box . . .

The colour of the entire universe and the whole of space
The whisper of the wind rolling through the trees
The first wave of the first sea there ever was

My box is fashioned from gold, silk and satin
With silver on the lid and diamonds in the corners.
Its hinges are made of the finest wood ever.

I will surf on my box to the ends of the Earth
And the whole world.

Daniella Ndzi (9)
St Swithun's RC Primary School, Southsea

My Magic Box
(Based on 'Magic Box' by Kit Wright)

In my magic box I will keep . . .

The roar of a lion devastating everyone
The cold mist of the Antarctic shelf
The flames of a fire the size of a blue whale

In my magic box I will keep . . .

All the water in the shimmering sea
The smoke from the last searing flame
A comet racing down from the skies

In my magic box I will keep . . .

The breath of the last human being
The bullet from the first gun ever fired
The gunpowder used in the Guy Fawkes' plot

In my magic box I will keep . . .

The brightest star in the universe
A footprint made by Big Foot
The shadow of a panther prowling in the night

My box is fashioned from blue crystals
And the bark of a tree and silver
With clouds in the sky, on the lid
And blood in the corners.
Its hinges are made of moon rocks.

I shall surf on my box in space and throw comets
And traverse the stars.

Oscar Addecott (9)
St Swithun's RC Primary School, Southsea

My Magic Box
(Based on 'Magic Box' by Kit Wright)
I will put in my box . . .

The first fresh breath of a new life,
The first initial wonky steps of a brown baby foal
And the first sparkle of an enchanted fairy
Spreading the word of magic.

I will put in my box . . .

The everlasting warmth from a child's laughter
Spreading happiness throughout the world,
And the swish of a mermaid's tail,
Reflecting the shine of the sun
Into the dark corners of the world.

I will put in my box . . .

The secrets of the world,
Unlocking all the magical histories there are to see,
A dragon breathing out flowers
And a bunny breathing out fire.

My box is fashioned from white, silk waves
And emeralds from the freshest ground of the highest mountain.
White doves still fluttering for freedom, so speedy you can't see.
A handle engraved with the signs of the lost world inside on the lid.
Fire from the last dragon locked in the highest tower on the corners.
Its hinges are made from the remains of the Iron Man.

I shall surf on my box
From the light of the day
Through the wonders of the world to the dark of night.

Alba Elezi (10)
St Swithun's RC Primary School, Southsea

Magic Box
(Based on 'Magic Box' by Kit Wright)

In my magic box I will have . . .

A tooth attached to the most elegant necklace of all,
The shimmering syrup from Canada
And the mysterious sound of a bird singing its heart out.
The happiest Christmas Day ever.
In my magic box there will be
The whitest cliff of Dover there ever was.

My box will be fashioned from a lock of hair
From everyone I ever cared about.
In the corners I will have secrets
And fire from the Chinese dragon,
With the sun from the Caribbean on the lid.
Its hinges will be gold from the mines.
I shall surf on my box on the American sea.

Jessica Henshaw (9)
St Swithun's RC Primary School, Southsea

The Magic Box
(Based on 'Magic Box' by Kit Wright)

I will put in my box . . .

A witch on a golden and blue fish
And a super dog snack
Smacking my back.

I will put in my box . . .

The ice cream melting
In the hot, yellow sun.
The fat cow that had a heart attack
In the bedroom.
My box is fashioned from ice and silk
And pretty rocks
With chicken soup on the lid
And sugar in the corners.
Its hinges are dark chocolate and mushroom.

Selina Briggs (9)
St Swithun's RC Primary School, Southsea

The Magic Box
(Based on 'Magic Box' by Kit Wright)

In my box I will keep . . .

The sound of a barbaric lion, roaring as loud as he can.
The sharp teeth of a great white when it's ripped its prey to shreds.
A football that never goes flat, even if you make a hole in it.

In my box I will keep . . .

A friend that never argues with me.
The last laugh of a laughing leprechaun.
The last bullet ever fired in World War II.

In my magic box I shall keep . . .

A photo of my family that flies around with me.
The fiery scale of a fierce dragon.
The shining sword of a Hobbit.

My box is fashioned from silver and leather
And a leprechaun's hat,
With shrapnel on the lid and Hobbits in the corners.
Its hinges are made out of bullets.

I shall surf on my box through the Amazon
And the jungles of Asia.

Patrick Cregan (9)
St Swithun's RC Primary School, Southsea

The Calmness In The Cat

The calmness in the cat is white,
You only see it when it bites.
The calmness in it makes it playful,
So there's no need for it to sleep in a cradle.
As it scratches
Its nails feel like matches.
After that you get lots of cats,
Shortly later you get a craze for nuts.

Diarmid Becker (10)
St Thomas Garnet's School, Bournemouth

My Brothers

Mess makers
Toy breakers
They argue all the time
Fusspots
Smell lots
They never admit the crime

Cute faces
Nutcases
They're always covered in grime
Laugh loads
Little toads
They're little brothers
And they're mine.

Georgia MacDonald-Taylor (9)
St Thomas Garnet's School, Bournemouth

Shark, Look Out!

Fierce, hungry
Scary, frightening
Horrifying
White, sharp teeth.

Curvy fin, look out!
Before he bites you
Out of your skin.

When you go for a swim
Always look out
For his cheeky grin.

Matthew Landi (8)
St Thomas Garnet's School, Bournemouth

The Night Sky

The sky grows dark
and the moon comes out
and the wolf howls in the wind.

On top of cliffs and in the sea
dolphins jump into
the cold, cold wind.

As I sleep the flowers curl
and in the morning
they crisp and die.

Next day the autumn wind
catches my face
and I think of the night sky.

Eleanor Austin (11)
St Thomas Garnet's School, Bournemouth

Winter

Summer is fading fast
and the leaves turn to brown,
soon it will be winter
and the leaves will all fall down.

The days will shorten
and the jackets will get thicker,
Christmas will come
and so will the vicar.

Presents for the children
church at 10.30,
then out into the snow
till we are frozen and dirty.

Theodore Jeffries (10)
St Thomas Garnet's School, Bournemouth

Anger Is . . .

Anger is homework.
Anger is reading a book.
Anger is having a shower.
Anger is Dad singing in the shower.
Anger is going shopping with Mum.
Anger is cleaning your room.
Anger is getting shouted at.
Anger is no playtime.
Anger is spelling.
Anger is Dad's smelly car.
Anger is writing this.

Eva Becker (8)
St Thomas Garnet's School, Bournemouth

House

Once there was an old, old house
Found in a haunted wood
Three storeys high
Now all that's left is where the old house stood.

Once a pan stood bubbling on a stove
A fire burning in the grate
Two children in this house
Knew no hate.

Yasmin Sabih (11)
St Thomas Garnet's School, Bournemouth

The Boat

I love the way that the boat goes swiftly along the surface.
I love the way that the engine goes round and round.
I love the blast of the foghorn.
I love the waves crashing against the boat.
I love it when I can see the boat on the horizon.

Emile Sabih (8)
St Thomas Garnet's School, Bournemouth

My Dog

My dog likes everything,
But my cats don't like him.
He licks everything,
Even me!
When I take him out for walks
He almost tramples down the house.
I call him Dogey,
But my brother calls him Frogey Dogey,
Because he tramples down the floor!
He can run at 100mph.
He zooms past me on my bike!

Kai Groves-Waters (7)
St Thomas Garnet's School, Bournemouth

The Lazy Dog

My dog is so lazy.
His colour is white.
He lays all day on the floor.
He gets fatter and fatter every single day.
Every week he goes outside on the grass
And sleeps in the sun all day.
The only thing that moves is his ears.
That's my lazy dog.

Kaan Beskardes (10)
St Thomas Garnet's School, Bournemouth

Raining

It's raining, it's raining, hip hip hooray.
It's raining, it's raining, let's go and play.
It's raining, it's raining, *drip, drip* on my head.
It's raining, it's raining, now it's time for bed.

Scott Austin (8)
St Thomas Garnet's School, Bournemouth

Legend Of The Dragon

When the lights all went out,
No one stays about,
Apart from a harmless poor dog,
Who got caught up in the fog
And is stuck there for good,
And had to face the legend dragon in the hood.
The dragon dies in sunlight and comes back in the night,
To find anything left to fight.

Dominic Hughes (10)
St Thomas Garnet's School, Bournemouth

My Favourite Hobby

I have a favourite hobby
to play this pleases me,
it's silver, long and shiny,
the flute fills me with glee.

I learn to play at school
and in a band I play,
all sorts of different music,
I practise every day.

Rebecca Giddens (10)
St Thomas Garnet's School, Bournemouth

Fruits

Apples are green
Apples are red
Apples are mean
As big as my head.

Pears are yummy
I could score them in my tummy
They are cool
I could eat them all.

Taylor Rees-Wilton (10)
St Thomas Garnet's School, Bournemouth

The Castle

Down in the deep, deep forest,
Where the leaves are lush and green,
There stands a huge old castle,
Where nobody's ever been.

A tattered door creaks open,
A ghostly face appears,
Scared, I scream and run away,
Not to be seen for a million years.

Jessica Balfour (10)
St Thomas Garnet's School, Bournemouth

My Favourite Pony

Honey is my favourite pony,
Her back is very, very bony.
I love to groom and tack her up,
She is really like a big cuddly pup.
I like to ride on her back,
But if it's raining I wear my mac.
I love Honey and she loves me,
So one day I am going to ask her to tea!

Amelia Wood Power (9)
St Thomas Garnet's School, Bournemouth

Midnight

Get out of bed
Face fully red.
Midnight, the coldest time of day
Right in the middle of May.
Bump my head on the floor
I just can't take anymore.
All I'm trying to say
Is aliens are invading today.

Daniel Tofangsazan (10)
St Thomas Garnet's School, Bournemouth

My Birthday Pet

This morning my mum did surprisingly say
A pet I could have for my birthday.
'I am so excited,' I shout out loud,
Which pet shall I choose that will make me proud?

A fluffy rabbit or perhaps a duck?
A goldfish or a hamster for luck?
Some gerbils or a furry cat,
But not a dormouse, who will sleep on the mat.

Perhaps a horse that will roam in the field
Or a hive of bees, some honey to yield?
I have now decided, it's as small as a cup,
My final decision is to buy a pup!

Matthew Giddens (10)
St Thomas Garnet's School, Bournemouth

Pickle

Pickle is one of my dogs.
He likes jumping over logs.

He likes to chew bones,
But turns his nose up at ice cream cones!

Pickle is very funny,
When you rub his tummy.

He wiggles his legs,
Then sits up and begs.

I love my dog Pickle.
It's great, he likes a tickle!

Piers Verstage (9)
St Thomas Garnet's School, Bournemouth

Dumpty Humpty

Dumpty Humpty sat on a door
Then he slipped and fell to the floor,
It never hurt him - and yet it was fun
A few people came in, then everyone.

Everybody tried to climb up the door
Then everyone jumped and fell to the floor,
It was so fun they did it again - and again,
And again and again, until then . . .

The room shook a violent shudder,
Everybody shouted at each other,
The door fell inwards, the fun was gone,
They saw the next door and all jumped on.

Nicholas Beaumont (9)
St Thomas Garnet's School, Bournemouth

The Summer Sun

The summer sun, shining so bright
it is like having a night with no sight.
The trees say hello and the sun says hay
on a such a beautiful day.
They say if you look at such a sunny day
you should go outside and play.
So go outside in the bright summer sun
and I can tell you, it's really fun.
Jump and run in the grass all day
it's better than eating a bun.
All day, play, play, every single day
I say play, play, play, play every single *day*.

Hibba Herieka (8)
St Thomas Garnet's School, Bournemouth

Football

I have a heavy football.
Every time I kick it
It doesn't budge!
Once I took it to the park.
It knocked down every tree.
The birds in the trees
Flew for their lives
And stayed in the air till Christmas Eve.
When I got home
I said to myself,
I do not like this football.
So I went to the shop
Got myself a new one
And happily kicked it around in the garden.
Argh! It's heavy again!

Glenn Balfour (7)
St Thomas Garnet's School, Bournemouth

Little Blue Riding Wolf

Little Blue Riding Wolf
rode to town,
on the way he met a clown,
the clown was dressed in blue and white,
he held a stick of dynamite,
Little Blue Riding Wolf quickly turned,
the fuse on the stick had nearly burned,
the clown decided to save the day
and threw the dynamite into the bay.

Little Blue Riding Wolf thanked the clown
and . . . hand in hand they left the town.

Thomas Adams (9)
St Thomas Garnet's School, Bournemouth

Flory

Flory is my dog's name.
When she is naughty she turns in fame.
My dog is very cheeky indeed.
She runs around the field at shooting speed.
She leaps in the forest
And I laugh like mad!
When we lose her I am very, very sad.
I was having breakfast and she wanted the milk.
I gave it to her and stained my golden T-shirt, made of silk.
I love my dog very much,
I would hate it if she was in a hutch!
I would like to cuddle up to my dog
Then go out in the cold where you all see fog.

Olivia Adams (7)
St Thomas Garnet's School, Bournemouth

My Pet Roly

I have a pet called Roly.
He's very funny indeed.
He runs down the garden,
Like a bullet with his speed.
I really like my pet,
He's as cute as you could need.
I see him nearly every day.
He's very dirty indeed!
I love Roly very much.
I just can't leave him.
It's true.

Lily Newton (7)
St Thomas Garnet's School, Bournemouth

On Christmas Day

On Christmas Day
Excitedly everybody
Opens their presents
And says thank you
To God and Santa Claus
Who brings us the toys.
That makes it special,
On Christmas Day,
At last!

Stephania Robbins (7)
St Thomas Garnet's School, Bournemouth

Santa Claus

Whenever I walk down the road
It is a beautiful sight.
But it's night
And I look up at the sky,
The snow falls.
If I believe in fairies, angels and mermaids
Then I believe in Santa Claus
Because Santa Claus is coming to town.

Kira Allum (7)
St Thomas Garnet's School, Bournemouth

Lion

Lions are dangerous cats,
They eat any meat they find.
They squelch through the jungle,
Fighting every time.
Their sharp claws swishing in the air.
I'd like to be a lion,
Swishing my tail all around.

Howard Winsten-Korver (7)
St Thomas Garnet's School, Bournemouth

Himpy, Himpy

I have a dog called Himpy,
he's very kind and soft.

He's got a collar with doggy prints on
and a very shiny nose.

He's very cute and fun to be with
and very gentle too.

He sleeps on my bed the whole night through,
Himpy, you are my very best friend.

Aiden O'Sullivan (7)
St Thomas Garnet's School, Bournemouth

School Trip

I went on my school trip
I went to a museum
I saw dinosaurs
I wanted to stay overnight
But then it was time to go
When I got home
I drew a picture
I put it up in my bedroom window.

Gina Davis (7)
St Thomas Garnet's School, Bournemouth

Orang-utan

Orang-utans swinging from branch to branch.
Eating bananas on the way.
Chattering and splashing,
Eating as they go.
Eating fruit and peeling bananas.
People think they are cheeky.
I definitely agree!

Finlay Padwick (7)
St Thomas Garnet's School, Bournemouth

Night

Every single night
I go to sleep and curl up tight.
I try to think of a story
But it is always about a fight.
Next thing I knew, one night
I was thinking about a light.
I thought it was a special light
Because it seemed so bright.
Soon it was breakfast time
So once more I slept all night!

Sophie Sawyer (7)
St Thomas Garnet's School, Bournemouth

My Cat

My cat licks every time he's happy.
He licks me in the garden
And when he's very angry.
But when I draw a portrait
There's footprints all over it.
I usually wonder why my cat licks
But best of all I love my cat
Whatever he does!

Lucy Taylor (7)
St Thomas Garnet's School, Bournemouth

Tiger

The colour of the tiger is black and orange.
You can see his amber eyes twinkle in the sunlight.
He prowls through the long grass that camouflages his stripes
But he will give you a fright with his fierce teeth
And his heavy jaw, ready to bite!

Jonty Hughes (9)
St Thomas Garnet's School, Bournemouth

Hairy House

Once there was a hairy house.
No one lived there except a mouse.
His name was Henry
And to his friends he was very friendly.

But one day a family moved in,
Henry thought this was the end of him.
They might know he was there and set a trap,
He had no time to take a nap.

The hairy house came to his aid
And said, 'Come outside into the shade.
You can live with me instead
And make my leaves a comfy bed.'

So this poem comes to an end,
Henry Mouse and his hairy friend!

Tallulah Pollard (9)
St Thomas Garnet's School, Bournemouth

Karate

I go to karate every day
I punch, block and kick
I'm the best at karate
When we do challenges.
I win all the time
By the way
When karate is finished
I don't care,
I go and fight with my sister!

Nikan Motlagh (7)
St Thomas Garnet's School, Bournemouth

Max, My Twin

Max is my brother, who looks like me
But my name is Fin, as twins are we
Our teacher at school is the biggest sin
As I become Max and he becomes Fin
We don't mind, we think it's funny
Like mixing salt and pepper, milk and honey
So please Mrs Carnell don't be blue
If Max and I call you Mrs Crew!

Findlay Purchase (9)
Salway Ash CE (VA) Primary School, Bridport

Red Devil Rooney

Red Devil Rooney runs down the pitch
Dribbling the ball without a hitch
He looks up, the goal is in sight
Kicks the ball with all his might
The crowd stop and hold their breath
As the keeper stands white as death
Past his ear and into the net
15-0, the best goal yet!

Max Purchase (9)
Salway Ash CE (VA) Primary School, Bridport

Silence

Silence feels fluffy like my slippers
Silence is blue like the bright blue sky.
Silence sounds quiet like a drop of water falling from the sky.
Silence tastes like creamy ice cream.
Silence glows like the silver moon.

Georgia Walther (7)
Salway Ash CE (VA) Primary School, Bridport

Water Fountain

Water fountain, water fountain
feels like a cold mountain.

Water fountain, water fountain
tastes like a blackberry mountain.

Water fountain, water fountain
smells like a rose mountain.

Water fountain, water fountain
looks like a golden mountain.

Water fountain, water fountain
sounds like a buzzing mountain.

Water fountain, water fountain
glows like a star mountain.

Jamie Herbert (7)
Salway Ash CE (VA) Primary School, Bridport

Anger

Anger is a pool of fire,
It is like exploding your head with pressure,
It sounds like a Cyclops destroying a city,
It smells like fire burning down a building,
It tastes like burning hot lava.

Jamie Rocha (8)
Upton Junior School, Poole

Silence

Silence smells like a field of fresh green grass.
It sounds like an open, empty room.
It tastes like frozen air with no taste.
Silence feels like a big gust of wind!

Tommy Hughes (8)
Upton Junior School, Poole

My Celebrations

I celebrate
The sight of my Christmas tree
It lights up the lounge.

I celebrate
The sound of people laughing and running
Into the cold sea

I celebrate
The taste of ice cream with chocolate sauce
It always cheers me up a lot.

I celebrate
The smell of Christmas
With all the Christmas candles lit.

I celebrate
The memory of when I got my puppy Gus
He's so, so cute.

I celebrate
The feel of my Christmas decorations
They're so pretty on the tree.

I love Christmas.

Jasmin Doe (9)
Upton Junior School, Poole

Hunger

Hunger is like some empty dishes.
It is like an empty, dark cottage with spiders on the floor.
It smells like a dark cloud with rain about to burst.
It tastes like darkened, dirty water.
It sounds like the thunder rumbling.
It feels like the whole wide world has stopped in your tracks.
It looks like there's only one person on Earth - you.

Tara Prince (9)
Upton Junior School, Poole

Silence

Silence smells like an empty cupboard.
Silence tastes like an empty dustbin.
Silence sounds like it's no one in bed with you.
Silence is like feeling a silent door.
Silence is like you are on your own.
Silence is like your door is closed
And you and your brother are not in, or your sister.

Silence tastes like no one is in your house.
Silence tastes like you're lost in a forest.
Silence tastes like you're in a coach on your own.
Silence is like a cat has gone.

Silence is like a school that is working.
Silence is like a class that is silent reading.
Silence is a school that is silent.
Silence is a silent playground.
Silence is a quiet swimming class.

Silence is like a silent toilet room.
Silence is a quiet car park.
Silence is a quiet playground.
Silence is a quiet rec.

Christopher Masters (8)
Upton Junior School, Poole

Happiness

Happiness is like children skipping in the playground.
Happiness sounds like feet tapping as people
                               run about the playground.
Happiness smells like fresh air.
Happiness tastes like a milkshake in the morning.
Happiness is like flowers looking up to a blue sky.
Happiness is like children splashing in puddles on a rainy day.

Eve Collins (8)
Upton Junior School, Poole

Love

Love is like a bright bursting flame
It is like the tickle of a butterfly.

Love sounds like a calm, sweet whisper
And the *coo coo* of a freshly hatched bird.

Love tastes like your favourite toy
You can keep it forever.

Love looks like a huge pink volcano
Bubbling with love.

Love feels like the great power of the sun
Warming you bit by bit!

Seven Mason (8)
Upton Junior School, Poole

Darkness

Darkness is like a big dark room.
Darkness is like lurking outside at night.
Darkness is like a candle that has been blown out.
Darkness is like me turning the light switch off.
Darkness is like being locked in a cupboard.
Darkness is like me closing my eyes.
Darkness is like being in a big box.

Luis Hayes (8)
Upton Junior School, Poole

Love

It sounds like colourful children playing together.
It smells like lovely strawberry lipstick.
It tastes like a lovely juicy apple or crunchy chocolate.

Kieran Higson (8)
Upton Junior School, Poole

Darkness

Darkness is like a pitch-black chalkboard
Darkness is like a blackboard pen scribbled all over you
Darkness tastes like a piece of sugar paper
Darkness smells like a sweet chocolate biscuit
Darkness sounds like a clown blowing through the trees
Darkness smells like a candle just blown out
Darkness is like a chess piece on the board
Darkness sounds like a hummingbird in the trees
Darkness feels like an ice cold breeze in the air
Darkness smells like a chocolate cake with a cherry on the top
Darkness is like the moon!

Sam Venner (8)
Upton Junior School, Poole

Love

It's like someone hugging you.
Like someone is always hanging around with you.
Somebody kissing you all day.
Sounds like someone singing a love song.
Smells like strawberries and orange.
Tastes like smelly flowers.

Lewis Fooks (8)
Upton Junior School, Poole

Love

Love is like a creamy amazing cake.
Love is like one hundred kisses.
Love sounds like fresh air blowing through my ear.
Love smells like fresh green grass.
Love tastes like a whole lot of happiness.

Lauren Bown (8)
Upton Junior School, Poole

Things I Like Best

I celebrate
The sight of pretty birds
Shooting through the air
So quick you can't see them.

I celebrate
The sound of the wind
Blowing those rainy clouds away.

I celebrate
The feel of my toy tiger
So soft and cuddly.

I celebrate
The taste of warm chocolate
So warm it melts in your mouth.

I celebrate
The memory of the night
We brought our dog home
So soft and silky.

I celebrate
The day my little brother was born
So tiny, so sweet.

I celebrate
The colour of red
Always will keep me warm
Something I'll treasure forever.

Jamie-Leigh Simpson (9)
Upton Junior School, Poole

Love

Love sounds like fresh air
It looks like clouds
It looks like happiness
It smells like flowers in the sky.

Ella Upward (8)
Upton Junior School, Poole

My Celebration Poem

I celebrate
The sight of the stars
Sparkling in the night sky
Like a candle being lit.

I celebrate
The sound of whiteboard pens
As they squeak across the whiteboard.

I celebrate
The feel of my pencil case
As I rub my hand against it
Like chocolate melting in my mouth.

I celebrate
The taste of Mini Cheddars
When my tongue gets round it.

I celebrate
The memory of the first time at school
As nervous as can be
Like the first time in a Ferrari.

I celebrate
The colour of light blue
As it reminds me of Christmas time.

I celebrate
My friendship of my friend and I
Making my head go *bang!*
Because she is so special.

Ella Smith (10)
Upton Junior School, Poole

Anger

Anger is like a bulldozer hitting you.
It tastes like poison ivy gushing inside your throat.
It smells like a hint of darkness going through you
And that's what anger is all about.

Rachel King
Upton Junior School, Poole

The Praise Poem

I celebrate
The sight of the froth of the sea
Crashing against the dry sand of the beach.

I celebrate
The sound of a football
As it hits the back of the net.

I celebrate
The feel of my bed duvet
As I cuddle it and fall asleep.

I celebrate
The taste of chocolate
As it melts inside my mouth.

I celebrate
The memory of my first word
As it came out of my tiny mouth.

Lewis Kelly (10)
Upton Junior School, Poole

Celebration Poem

I celebrate
The sight of Arsenal playing football
They are like monsters running about
Skilful with the ball

I celebrate
The sound of people cheering Arsenal
When they score a goal

I celebrate
The rubber for the white board
Squashy and soft

I celebrate
Smooth melting chocolate
Mixed with smashed up Smarties.

Sam Jones (9)
Upton Junior School, Poole

Celebration Poem

I celebrate
The sight of baby foxes
Trotting down the street
With their fluffy tails wagging.

I celebrate
The sound of cockatiels
Squawking in their cage.

I celebrate
The feel of cats
Purring with soft fur.

I celebrate
The taste of apple juice
Trickling down my throat.

I celebrate
The memory of baby hedgehogs
Eating all the slugs
In my garden with their spikes.

Joshua Brewster (9)
Upton Junior School, Poole

What Is The Moon?

The moon is a white ball being kicked up high.
It is a white blob of paint on black paper.
It is a dinghy sailing on the dark sea.
It is a milk bottle top on the black floor.
It is snow on mountain tops.
It is white chocolate melting in a blue bowl.
It is a white scarf rolled up into a ball.
It is a rubber on some black carpet.
It is a piece of paper floating in the air.

Kaylee Gunner (9)
Upton Junior School, Poole

Things I Celebrate

I celebrate
The sight of the sun shining in the sky
So bright that I can't keep my eyes open in my back garden

I celebrate
The sound of my rabbits thumping
In their hutches

I celebrate
The feel of my rabbit's fur
Soft, furry and grey

I celebrate
The taste of cottage pie
With my drink of milk

I celebrate
The memory of when my friend left
And the good things we did together
But I still remember

I celebrate
The colour of my rabbits in their hutches
One grey, one black.

Catherine Lenton (9)
Upton Junior School, Poole

My Speedy Race Car

My race car looks like a relaxing car cake.
He sounds like a ginormous, roaring dinosaur
thundering in an enormous jungle.
Hotshot is his name!
He tastes like me sprinting on the icy grass.
My race car smells like flaming petrol
bubbling up and down in a huge jet.
He feels as smooth as a car's tyre speeding along the road.
Hotshot is the fastest race car in the world.

Miles Mitchinson (8)
Upton Junior School, Poole

Things I Celebrate

I celebrate
The sight of my hamster
Whizzing around his wheel
Like his tail was on fire.

I celebrate
The sound of Star Wars movies
With massive blaster battles.

I celebrate
The feel of a warm bath
All on my own.

I celebrate
The taste of a steak and kidney pie
With the warm crust round my mouth.

I celebrate
The memory of going into school
Going in with confidence
For the first time.

Linus Head (9)
Upton Junior School, Poole

My Magical Pony

My pony sounds like the wind shaking the earth.
It reminds me of my baby brother's birth.

My pony looks like the dark night sky
Blue and sparkly white.

My pony feels like fluffy black fur
From a tame bear.

My pony smells like strawberries
All red, bright and new.

My pony tastes like chocolate pudding
Served on a golden plate.

Jessica Wyatt (7)
Upton Junior School, Poole

Celebration Poem

I celebrate
The sound of the rain
Pitter-pattering on the windowpane.

I celebrate
The sound of
Leaves on a windy day.

I celebrate
The feel of cats purring at me
When I am asleep.

I celebrate
The taste of squash
In a glass.

I celebrate
The colour of the rainbow
Glistening in the sky with lots of colours.

Emily Jellett (9)
Upton Junior School, Poole

What Is The Sea?

The sea is a beautiful silk bed
Glistening in the sun.

The sea is the queen of vast lands
Ruling the boats she does.

The sea is a corruption of the world
Making floods when she smiles.

The sea is a home for many
Helping them survive.

The sea is a treasure chest
Filled with gold coins.

The sea is a graveyard
For people from the past.

Becky Driscoll (10)
Upton Junior School, Poole

The Things I Celebrate

I celebrate
The sight of the full moon
Shining and glittering in the midnight sky
And Martians hiding on the other side.

I celebrate
The sound of the owl
Tooting and tweeting in the darkness.

I celebrate
The feel of my dog's soft fur
Brushing against my face.

I celebrate
The taste of my grandma's shepherd's pie
Melting in my mouth.

I celebrate
The memory of my whole family
Eating delicious pizzas and watching TV.

I celebrate
The colour of blue
And the clear sky.

Thomas Pike (9)
Upton Junior School, Poole

Silence

Silence is like the world beginning,
the shimmery seas and trees running away.
The calm sea lashing onto my feet
with a hint of a cat's purr lying next to me.
It smells like chocolate milkshake
on my bedside table.
It tastes like strawberries
dipped into luscious thick cream!

Tamsin Edmondson (8)
Upton Junior School, Poole

I Celebrate

I celebrate
The sight of baby foxes
Crawling like a soft, tiny,
Brown mouse.

I celebrate
The sound of dogs
Barking to each other
Across the fields.

I celebrate
The feel of my dog
Crawling on my bed
Like a furry, ginger tiger.

I celebrate
The taste of dark chocolate
And the crunch of dark chocolate.

I celebrate
The memory of my 1st birthday
When I tasted that delicious,
Crunchy chocolate cake.

Katie Tilbury (9)
Upton Junior School, Poole

Anger

It sounds like two giants
stamping their feet.
It smells like thunder
crashing against the ground.
It tastes like some fire,
it burns up inside your mouth.

Sophie Phillips (8)
Upton Junior School, Poole

The Amazing Poem

I celebrate
The sight of snow
Slowly falling from the dark night sky.

I celebrate
The sound of pumpkins
Laughing evilly on the spooky shelf.

I celebrate
The feel of the waves
Hitting my legs, getting them soaked.

I celebrate
The taste of chocolate
Running down my tongue.

I celebrate
The memory of walking
My cute adorable cocker spaniels.

I celebrate
The colour of blue
On my bedroom wall.

James Murray (9)
Upton Junior School, Poole

Laughter

It sounds like someone laughing.
It feels like a feather touching my head.
It smells like toffee in the air.
It smells like a person playing the trumpet.
It tastes like spaghetti Bolognese.
It reminds me of the time when me
And my two brothers laughed our heads off.

Oscar Head (8)
Upton Junior School, Poole

Snowy Christmas

I celebrate
The sight of the glinting snowflakes
Falling through the sky.

I celebrate
The sound of the jingling reindeers
Glinting through the sky.

I celebrate
The feel of the crumbling Christmas pudding
In my soft hands.

I celebrate
The taste of the milky chocolate decorations
On the beautiful Christmas tree.

I celebrate
The memory of the snowballs
I throw at my annoying sister.

I celebrate
The colour of my sparkling Christmas
Wrapping paper from Santa.

Jonathan Hayward (9)
Upton Junior School, Poole

Hunger

Hunger's like an empty stomach with no bones in you
It sounds like my belly yawning
It smells like the wind blowing like fire
It tastes like when I swallow my tongue
Like a fireball
Hunger is like an empty tomb.

Lacey Cole (8)
Upton Junior School, Poole

The Greatest Poem Ever

I celebrate
The sight of my baby sister
Crawling on the rough sand
Picking up shells.

I celebrate
The sound of the dog next door
Howling at the bright moon.

I celebrate
The feel of new puppies' fur
Crawling on me.

I celebrate
The taste of Mum's cooked food
Drifting down the hallway.

I celebrate
The memory of new fishes
Swimming along the river
To some people throwing food.

Samuel Hirons (10)
Upton Junior School, Poole

Sadness

Sadness is like a friend hurting you.
It is like blood pouring down your clothes.
It sounds like a boy saying, 'Go away!'
It smells like the smoke choking you.
It sounds like wool in your mouth.

When someone is mean you have to tell the teacher.

Natalie Baker (8)
Upton Junior School, Poole

I Celebrate

I celebrate
The sight of the howling seas
That pull the golden sand away.

I celebrate
The sound of a purring tiger
While it's happily playing with a ball.

I celebrate
The feel of my purple pencil case,
The soft bumps of the fur.

I celebrate
The taste of a delicious chocolate doughnut
As it melts inside my mouth.

I celebrate
The memory of Christmas
As the food cooking steams up the window
And the way my mum cooks dinner!

Savannah Morgan (9)
Upton Junior School, Poole

My Magical Pony

My magical pony is happy and magical.
It has brown and grey feet.

My magical pony's name is Luck.
She is very kind when I'm not well.
She comes and snuggles on me.
She is very fair.

My magical pony is most beautifully soft,
Cheeky and funny.

Sian Grey (7)
Upton Junior School, Poole

I Celebrate

I celebrate
The sight of food in the cupboard
Stacking up high in the fridge
As high as a giraffe's neck.

I celebrate
The sound of brilliant music
Loud and clear like a trombone.

I celebrate
The feel of the radiator
Warming me like a pie.

I celebrate
The taste of chocolate
As it melts in my hands.

I celebrate
The memory of Christmas
And the presents under the Christmas tree.

I celebrate
The colour green
Reminding me of life
And grass and trees and flowering delight.

Cameron Wemyss (9)
Upton Junior School, Poole

My Pony

My pony is called Rosie
and she is the colour of rain.

She smells of strawberries
and ice cream.

She feels like a silky pillow.
She tastes like chocolate cake.
She sounds like the wind in a canter.

Chantelle Squibb (7)
Upton Junior School, Poole

Celebration Poem

I celebrate
The sight of Santa and his reindeers
Floating all around me.

I celebrate
The sound of ghosts
Zooming everywhere.

I celebrate
The feel of my dog Kouba
His rough tongue when he licks me.

I celebrate
The taste of chocolate
Melting in my mouth.

I celebrate
The memory of my hamster
When he squeaks his little voice at me.

Aaron Sheldon (9)
Upton Junior School, Poole

Laughter

Laughter sounds like a clucking hen.
Laughter feels like a fire.
Laughter smells like a hot fire.
Laughter looks like a chicken going mad.
Laughter tastes like burning toast.
Laughter reminds me of me going bonkers
when my brother tells me a joke.

Calum Driver (8)
Upton Junior School, Poole

I Celebrate

I celebrate
The sight of England playing rugby,
When they tackle they jump on each other.

I celebrate
The sound of high performance cars,
Like a rocket taking off.

I celebrate
The feel of a rugby ball,
Lumpy and rigid.

I celebrate
The taste of Chinese food and pasta,
It is yum.

I celebrate
The memory of my sister's leaving party
Because we were running about.

James Jackson (9)
Upton Junior School, Poole

Silence

Silence looks like the sun is setting behind the mountains.
Silence feels like fishes are floating through the air.
Silence sounds like birds singing softly.
Silence smells like red roses twirling around.
Silence tastes like fizzy drink swirling down my throat.
It reminds me of when silver stars are waving at me.

Nina Czarnokoza (9)
Upton Junior School, Poole

Ross' Masterpiece

I celebrate
The sight of my family
At Christmas.

I celebrate
The sound of rain
Patting on my window.

I celebrate
The feel of my soft cover
In the morning.

I celebrate
The taste of Christmas pudding
As the clock strikes twelve.

I celebrate
The memory of holidays
In the summer.

I celebrate
The colour of
The wide white sea.

Ross Higson (9)
Upton Junior School, Poole

Crazy

Crazy sounds like people screaming their heads off.
Crazy feels like building Lego.
Crazy smells like hot chocolate.
Crazy looks like dogs running around the house.
Crazy reminds me of panting.

Joe Musselwhite (9)
Upton Junior School, Poole

The Shining Moon

The moon is like
A white wolf in the night
On the highest rock.

The moon is like
Fresh milk in a sparkling bottle.

The moon is like
White snow on top of the mountains.

The moon is like
Melted milk chocolate.

The moon is like
A big grey boulder.

The moon is like
A white ball kicked up high.

The moon is like
A milk top on the black floor.

The moon is like
A sparkling eyeball.

The moon is like
A big fluffy cloud.

Harvey Nichols (9)
Upton Junior School, Poole

Happiness

Happiness is like a bird coming from the sky.
It feels like I'm going to be happy all day
And it smells like the air is really lovely.
It tastes like a packet of sweets coming from the sky.
It reminds me of a bird going cheep all the time.

Abigail Baker (8)
Upton Junior School, Poole

I Celebrate Things

I celebrate
The sight of Arsenal playing a football match
They look sweaty
Really skilful and are the best.

I celebrate
The sound of babies crying
When they have their nappies changed.

I celebrate
The feel of my next-door neighbour's dog and cat
They are really fluffy.

I celebrate
The taste of melting chocolate
Just been bought in the best shop ever.

I celebrate
The memory of when I was little
My dad gave me an ice cream
And I got it everywhere.

Abigail Smith (9)
Upton Junior School, Poole

Crazy

Crazy sounds like people are having fun.
Crazy feels like your hair standing up on your head.
Crazy smells like fresh air in the morning.
Crazy looks like people are having a brilliant time.
Crazy reminds me of very good parties.

Maddison Higson (8)
Upton Junior School, Poole

I Celebrate

I celebrate
The sight of a new moon
In the night's silent sky
And stars so bright, far, far away
In the sky like flickering candles.

I celebrate
The sound of singing birds
On the branches of the old oak
And the feel of my cat's furry fur
Rubbing gently against my face.

I celebrate
The taste of my bubbly hot chocolate
And the fruity peaches on my cold lips.

I celebrate
A bonfire on a cold winter's night
And a flower on a warm summer's day.

Chloe Bennett (9)
Upton Junior School, Poole

Excitement

Excitement sounds like me rustling my presents on my birthday.
Excitement feels like it is going to be my birthday all over again.
Excitement smells like chocolate on my birthday cake.
Excitement looks like my big sister watching TV.
Excitement tastes like my birthday cake sliding down my throat.
Excitement reminds me of Christmas Eve.

Zara Benjafield (8)
Upton Junior School, Poole

Sandy Beaches

I celebrate
The sight of sand, golden and brown
And girls playing volleyball on the beach and the sand dunes.

I celebrate
The sound of the waves crashing
The sound of girls screaming how cold the sea is.

I celebrate
The feel of girls crashing into me
And the sea going and never stopping.

I celebrate
The taste of sand sandwiches on my tongue
And the sea water crashing in my mouth.

I celebrate
The memory of my head in the sea
And of the girls chasing after me all the way home.

James Craze (10)
Upton Junior School, Poole

Worried

Worried sounds like your mum
Crying after a bad argument.

Worried feels like pain
And your dad telling you off.

Worried looks like a tree in pain
Because it is being cut down.

Worried smells like it is a rainy sky
Dripping on you.

Worried reminds you
Of when your mum and dad
Have had an argument
And everybody cries.

Molly Lloyd (8)
Upton Junior School, Poole

Fun

Fun sounds like laughter from the fair.
It smells like a tub of fish and chips.
It tastes like a bucket of candy.
It feels like I'm on a roller coaster.
It looks like a store of candy.

Connel Duffy (8)
Upton Junior School, Poole

Sleeping Football

Once there was a sleeping football
It slept all day
If you tried to kick it
It felt like hard clay.

Laying in the mud all day
People playing rugby
Breaking their footy bootees
It's another Sunday.

Kick it with no shoes on
Your toes will surely break
Pick it up and carry it
Sell it at a fete.

Stephen Brain (7)
Upton Junior School, Poole

My Kitty

My kitten is called Jesper, she is very cute
She is black and white like clouds and thunder.
She tastes like strawberries
She smells like roses growing in the sun
She sounds like a baby crying.

Chloe Cole (7)
Upton Junior School, Poole

Husky And Wolf

My husky and wolf
Are as beautiful as a star.

My husky is called Lily
My wolf is called Emily.

My husky and wolf howl
Like a falling star hitting Earth.

Their paws are made of crystals
And their noses smell of toffee crumble.

They feel like velvet and cotton wool
And their eyes are like dancing angels.

Their teeth sparkle of drool
In the sunlight.

My husky and wolf listen
Like students listening to their teacher.

Jessica Upton (7)
Upton Junior School, Poole

Happiness

Happiness is the bright colour of blue.
Blue is the meaning of helpful and kind.

Happiness is like children playing in the sun.
Happiness is like chocolate cake and cream.

Happiness means people with good manners.
Happiness means smiling and laughing.

I like happiness because you have a very good time!

Kasey Taylor (8)
Upton Junior School, Poole

My Magical Pony

My pony looks like the moon
All shiny and bright
Up so high in the sky
On a cold winter's night.

My pony sounds like the wind
Shaking the Earth
And reminds me of my
Baby brother's birth.

My pony tastes like vanilla ice cream
And strawberries so sweet
All dished up in a bowl
With her mane all brushed neat.

My pony smells like fresh hay
In a barn so clean
My pony is very gentle
And is never ever mean.

My magical pony feels like cotton wool
All fluffy and white
In the sun sparkling
Very, very bright.

Bryony Hobden (8)
Upton Junior School, Poole

Anger

Anger sounds like blood dripping
From someone who has just got shot.
It feels like you're bursting with explosion.
It smells like the anger is there right in front of you.
It looks like a big ball of pouring fire.
It tastes like knives stabbing through my toe.
It reminds me of lots and lots of screaming and shouting.

Elle-Rose Arnold (8)
Upton Junior School, Poole

Hyper Mad

I once met a boy in the playground
Who was going hyper mad.
I asked what he was doing?
He replied,
'Bodebad!'

I once met a boy in the cloakroom
Who was spinning around and around.
I asked him what he was doing?
He replied,
'Wowwowwow!'

I once met a boy in the classroom
Who was pulling faces at me.
I asked him what he was doing?
He replied,
'Hehewewe!'

I once met a boy in the library
Who was ripping books apart.
I asked him what he was doing?
He replied,
'Whatart!'

Jordan Mackenzie (8)
Upton Junior School, Poole

My Dogs

My dogs are big and fat
Comfy and tough
They're like a bar of chocolate

Their names are Cass and Kaizer
Their ears are floppy
They protect me like soldiers.

Madison Gossling (7)
Upton Junior School, Poole

Hate

Hate is when I get the blame
Hate is when my sister bites my hip
Hate is when my sister smacks my bum
Hate is my sister's attitude
Hate is my sister waking me up at 5.30am.

Ashley Pope (8)
Upton Junior School, Poole

Silence

Silence sounds like nothing is around me, it's just me.
Silence feels like you are lonely.
Silence looks like you're in a quiet place.
Silence tastes like books.

Morgan Tutt (8)
Upton Junior School, Poole

Car

Superstorm is a BMW car
Fast, speedy with a thunder sound
He's faster than his friends
He goes around bends
His best friend is called Ben.

Jordan Fripp (7)
Upton Junior School, Poole

Lego Star Wars

You get a person called Obi-Wan Kenobe
You get Master Yoda too
You get Obi-Wan's lightsaber
It is the colour blue.

Robert Beck (8)
Upton Junior School, Poole

Mad

My dad is so glad.
He steals my skateboard.
Why is he so bad?
I think he's *mad!*

I met a boy in a supermarket.
He's called Chad.
He looks bad.
He tried to take me home with him.
Is he *mad?*

I met a lad in a street.
He's holding a pad.
He looks sad.
I wonder if he's *mad?*

So what am I?
Am I sad?
Am I bad?
So am I *mad?*

Cameron Sinden (8)
Upton Junior School, Poole

My Nightmare

Nightmares are like falling out of a car
Sometimes I really think I'm going to get hurt.

Nightmares are tapping sounds on your window
Dare I look outside?

Nightmares are being very scared
Not knowing if it's real.

Daniel Meacham (8)
Upton Junior School, Poole

Young Writers Information

We hope you have enjoyed reading this book - and that you will continue to enjoy it in the coming years.

If you like reading and writing poetry drop us a line, or give us a call, and we'll send you a free information pack.

Alternatively if you would like to order further copies of this book or any of our other titles, then please give us a call or log onto our website at
www.youngwriters.co.uk

**Young Writers Information
Remus House
Coltsfoot Drive
Peterborough
PE2 9JX**

(01733) 890066